# Preah Khan Monastic Complex

# Preah Khan Monastic Complex

*Angkor, Cambodia*

Essays by Michael D. Coe, Olivier Cunin, Claude Jacques,
Christophe Pottier, Dawn F. Rooney, John H. Stubbs

Edited by Michael D. Coe and John H. Stubbs

This volume is published to celebrate two decades of architectural
conservation work at the temple of Preah Khan

World Monuments Fund is grateful to the Henry Luce Foundation
for its support of this volume

World Monuments Fund's publications are supported by the
Paul Mellon Endowment for Education

WORLD MONUMENTS FUND

SCALA

This edition © Scala Publishers Ltd 2011
Photographs and text © World Monuments Fund 2011

First published in 2011 by
Scala Publishers Ltd
Northburgh House
10 Northburgh Street
London EC1V 0AT
UK

ISBN: 978 1 85759 494 2

Project Editor: Sandra Pisano, Scala Publishers
Designer: Andrew Shoolbred
Copy Editor: Matthew Taylor
Printed and bound in China

10 9 8 7 6 5 4 3 2 1

All photographs courtesy of World Monuments Fund except:
pp. 19–26, 28, 29, 32–35 © Olivier Cunin
Front and back covers, pp. 2, 7, 9, 11, 30, 43, 46, 47 [right],
48, 79 © Sasha Constable
pp. 38, 51, 52, 53, 55 © EFEO, Paris
p. 56 © Meadows Museum, Shreveport, Louisiana

Every effort has been made to acknowledge correct copyright of images where
applicable. Any errors or omissions are unintentional and should be notified
to the Publisher, who will arrange for corrections to appear in any reprints.

FRONT COVER *Stupa* in the Central Sanctuary of Preah Khan
BACK COVER Preah Khan's Two-Storey Pavilion
FRONTISPIECE View between shrines in the south-west quadrant, Preah Khan
TITLE PAGE Drawing of *apsaras*, Hall of Dancers, Preah Khan, WMF
OVERLEAF RIGHT Carving of a Hindu ascetic figure fashioned from a prior seated
Buddha figure

# Contents

ព្រះរាជាណាចក្រកម្ពុជា
KINGDOM OF CAMBODIA

ជាតិ សាសនា ព្រះមហាក្សត្រ
NATION    RELIGION    KING

អាជ្ញាធរអប្សរា
A P S A R A

N° ........................

## Letter of Acknowledgement

Before Angkor was inscribed on the World Heritage List of UNESCO in 1992, a few international teams were carrying out the conservation and restoration projects at the site. The World Monuments Fund was one of the first teams that came to offer its participation in the efforts, by choosing to take care of one of the most prominent monuments of Cambodia: Preah Khan, erected during the late 12th century.

The World Monument Fund spent over a decade, since the early 1990s, dealing with the most urgent matters, of course, but also regularly maintaining the huge site. Reinforcing and stabilizing the weakened structures as well as clearing different ways obstructed by disorderedly piled-up blocks of stone are amongst the top priority work. The work, in brief, remakes the whole monument understandable by visitors. Without doubt, such an action is greatly worthy of praise.

Today, the World Monuments Fund proposes to us a collection of insightful studies related to several disciplines, dealing with the past as well as the present of the monument. The contributions come from eminent specialists. It is an honor for me to acknowledge this ultimate achievement on Preah Khan.

BUN Narith
Director-General
APSARA National Authority

# Introduction

Bonnie Burnham
President, World Monuments Fund

This publication celebrates 20 years of working at the temple of Preah Khan, one of the 40 Khmer temples at Angkor in Cambodia. With this publication, the urgent problems confronting the survival of this temple have been solved, but WMF remains engaged in the continuing maintenance of this beautiful site. Through this long association, we have come to feel a sense of parental responsibility, as well as pride, in its extraordinary qualities which are discovered by succeeding generations of visitors who continue to reveal themselves to us as our work continues.

When WMF first considered working at Angkor, there was no reliable information about the condition of the site. During the 1980s, visiting teams from India and Poland had begun the international effort to help Cambodia preserve this world-class cultural resource, but their work was not widely publicized. There were no international visitors to Angkor and the country was in a state of virtual isolation without either a telephone system or diplomatic relations with any country in the West. There was concern around the world about the condition of the monuments. Reports were published in the Western press erroneously suggesting that Angkor Wat had been completely destroyed by the Khmer Rouge.

It was in this environment that WMF fielded its first fact-finding mission to Angkor in late 1989. The team came back with the report that help was needed as soon a possible. Preah Khan was chosen as WMF's pilot project because of its lovely environmental qualities, with huge trees growing throughout the site, and partly because its challenges were relatively simple compared to the temple-pyramids of Angkor Wat and the Bayon. We wanted to start a training programme and the fact that Preah Khan had been a kind of academy in Khmer times, made it seem appropriate for our teaching mission.

In 1991, when the work began in earnest at Preah Khan, conditions in the country were far from stable. We were able, however, to recruit students from the Beaux Arts University in Phnom Penh to join us on the site and soon

Images in stone of a *dvarapala* (left) and *apsara* (right) in the shrine area of Preah Khan's north-west quadrant

WMF had a team of some 60 workers, overseen by seven student trainees and a small team of foreign advisors, enhanced occasionally with visiting specialists who were more than willing to offer advice in return for a visit to Angkor – which remained throughout the 1990s a place for the intrepid visitor only.

As our work evolved, from liberating the large site from the jungle, to developing low-technology conservation applications that would be workable in such an environment, to interpreting the site to increasing numbers of visitors, Cambodia also began to open to the world. Numerous international conservation teams from around the world joined WMF to assist Cambodia in the international conservation campaign launched by UNESCO in 1993 when Angkor became a World Heritage site. Today, Angkor is a premier tourist destination, bringing opportunities to the region and revenue to its still impoverished country. For WMF, Preah Khan remains a flagship, even though we have taken on new and greater challenges at other temples within the Angkor complex. Like Cambodia and its charming people, Preah Khan took our hearts. A leisurely stroll through the site is an opportunity for contemplation and reaffirms our belief that we made the right decisions, inspired by the serenity of the place itself, which was the most important quality to preserve.

Future generations of scholars, architectural historians and archaeologists will no doubt add to our knowledge of this richly evocative site with its 515 shrines and 72 *garuda* guardians. We are happy to have been part of this process and part of Preah Khan's history by ensuring its preservation. Now, with this publication, we are happy to share that learning experience.

# Learning from Angkor: An Archaeological Odyssey

Michael D. Coe

I first saw the world-renowned ruins of Angkor in late March 1954, as a very young man on my way home from a two-year government assignment in the Far East. It was at the height of the dry season, the heat was a bit overwhelming and the rice fields were nothing but brown stubble. While in Phnom Penh (then a lovely, sleepy French provincial town graced with a royal palace and Buddhist pagodas), I had luckily bought *Les Monuments du Groupe d'Angkor*, the wonderful, pocket-size guide (complete with maps) by Maurice Glaize. Armed with this, in the space of a week I made (as his book recommended) the *grand circuit*. I was transfixed by what I saw, not only by the architecture and the standing sculpture – much of which was still intact, including the heads of demons and gods on the *naga* balustrades of the causeways – but also by a profound sense of *déjà vu*: I had seen much the same vegetation (particularly silk-cotton trees and strangler figs) growing from the Maya ruins of Mexico and Central America. I had climbed Maya stepped temple-pyramids identical to Angkor's Baksei Chamkrong and slung my hammock in Maya rooms with the same corbel vaults as the ones at Angkor Wat and Preah Khan.

I had wanted to see Angkor ever since I had read about it as a teenager, so for me this was a dream come true. When I returned to my studies at Harvard, I bought and read every book on the subject that I could lay my hands on, particularly the magnificent reports by the archaeologists, art historians and epigraphers of the École Française d'Extrême-Orient (EFEO), who had been in charge of studying and restoring the great city since 1907. It was not only the amazing resemblance between two lowland, tropical forest civilizations – Maya and Khmer – that puzzled me, but also the disturbing disjunction between the Angkorian world of temples and palaces that the EFEO *savants* had described so well, and the lives of the ordinary Cambodians whom I had seen in the villages within and without the ancient city. What kind of a city was this? Where did such "ordinary" people actually live in the days of Suryavarman II and Jayavarman VII? Until the archaeological programmes of the last 15 years, such questions had no answers.

OPPOSITE Tree trunk engaged in Preah Khan's third enclosure wall, south-east quadrant

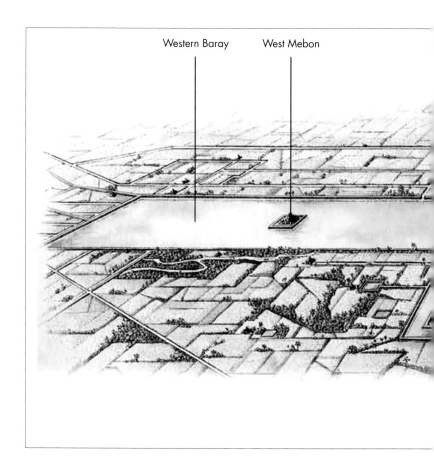

Western Baray    West Mebon

Although there are earlier remains within the limits of Angkor, such as indications of prehistoric circular villages, Angkor's history began on a day in the year 802 CE (two years after Charlemagne was anointed Holy Roman Emperor by the Pope), when a minor Khmer ruler known to us as Jayavarman II stood on a small temple-pyramid in the Kulen Hills of north-west Cambodia and took the title of *chakravartin*, "Universal Monarch". Descending to the plain just north of the Tonle Sap – the Great Lake – Jayavarman established his capital at Hariharalaya, about 10 kilometres to the east of present-day Siem Reap. Thus began the Khmer Empire, to become over the next five centuries the mightiest civilization of South-East Asia. After a succession of kings had ruled from Hariharalaya, one of these – Yashovarman I – moved the capital 15 kilometres to the north-west and named it Yashodarapura, "Glory-Bearing City", now known to us and to all the Khmer people as Angkor, "The City".

We might ask why Angkor is where it is. How did it become, in time, one of the world's greatest cities and the nodal point of an enormous Asian empire? The answer is that favourable geographic, geological and ecological factors all played a part. The city's centre (perhaps the temple-crowned hill known as Phnom Bakheng) lay just north of the Tonle Sap, a huge, shallow, freshwater lake that the monsoons of summer and early autumn cause to swell to four times its dry season size. As this inland sea begins to drain in late November, its waters become the world's most productive fishery per cubic metre. The receding waters expose fertile mudflats, on which farmers could sow and transplant the rice that was their staple food, a Nile-like situation that

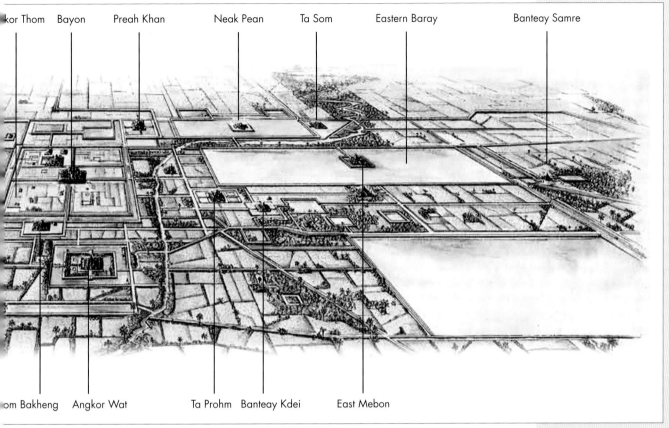

kor Thom  Bayon  Preah Khan  Neak Pean  Ta Som  Eastern Baray  Banteay Samre

om Bakheng  Angkor Wat  Ta Prohm  Banteay Kdei  East Mebon

Map of Angkor, looking north

produced the crops on which the entire state system of revenue and taxation ultimately depended.

The land between the Kulen uplands and the lake is a broad plain with extremely gentle relief. Aerial survey has disclosed traces of thousands of small, square, bounded rice paddies, which, while not as productive as the flood-recession fields, would have supplied ample rain-fed crops at the close of the wet season. Thanks to its high water table, it was easy to dig a *trapeang*, or pond, and we know from Zhou Daguang (a Chinese traveller of the late fourteenth century) that much of the population lived in proximity to these. But not far below these soils was one further resource for the Angkor state: brownish-red laterite, an ancient soil turned to stone, easily quarried and shaped before it hardens. It was laterite building blocks that formed the bases, platforms and cores of Angkor's temples and other structures, the protective walls surrounding all of Angkor's architectural complexes, and the corbel-vaulted bridges on its highways.

And lastly we have the Kulen Hills, to the north and east of the city. From sources on this limestone massif flowed all of the rivers and streams that fed Angkor's stupendous water management system, including its giant *barays* (reservoirs) and moats, to discharge finally into the Tonle Sap. The holiest of these streams was the Siem Reap river, identified by the Khmer with the Ganges of India; as it came down from the heights, its waters were sanctified by passing over carvings representing the creation of the universe and the male essence of the great Hindu god Shiva. From quarries in these hills came

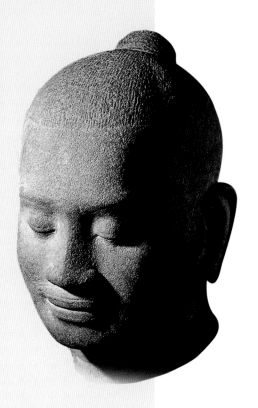

Jayavarman VII, Bayon Period

all of the fine sandstone from which were shaped the architectural blocks and facing stones of Angkor's building complexes, and the thousands of religious sculptures that once graced the city's temples.

Jayavarman II and Yashovarman I had chosen their site well.

Some very recent research has come up with answers to two major puzzles. First, what kind of city was this? And second, what was the function (or what were the functions) of the gigantic *barays*, with their millions of cubic metres of impounded water? The brilliant French archaeologist Bernard-Philippe Groslier proposed in 1979 that this was a "hydraulic city", in which the reservoirs provided water that was used to irrigate rice fields during the dry season, and he calculated that, because of this, up to two million souls could have dwelled in Angkor. This claim aroused spirited opposition from some geographers, who saw a purely ritual use for the *barays*, but excavations by the University of Sydney's Greater Angkor Project (GAP) and EFEO archaeologists have shown that at least in part Groslier was right: water *was* released in quantity to support year-round cultivation of rice.

Space-age technology, such as synthetic-aperture radar as applied by NASA over-flights, along with ground survey, has provided an overall picture of the settlement pattern of the entire city, which had a total extent of about 1,000 square kilometres. Most of it exhibits a low-density, dispersed-urban pattern similar to the far smaller royal cities of the lowland Classic Maya, such as Tikal and Calakmul, with (as Zhou had told us) the bulk of the population living in pile-supported wooden houses near *trapeangs*, or along roads and canals. Over this is a linear pattern oriented to the points of the compass, clearly imposed by the Angkor state: *barays*, roads and canals, moated, urban temple complexes such as Angkor Wat and Angkor Thom, monastic establishments, public buildings and plazas, and royal baths and pools.

One notable exception to this pattern of "urban sprawl" was Jayavarman VII's Angkor Thom, a moated and walled square covering 9 square kilometres. Its north-west quadrant was devoted to the royal palace, its occupants and thousands of functionaries and servants. Quite recently, the EFEO archaeologist Jacques Gaucher has carried out a complete survey of the jungle-covered south-east quadrant, proving this to be a densely occupied "downtown", with houses arranged in a grid pattern along a multitude of streets and canals. At least parts of Angkor Thom resembled the coeval, very crowded cities of China and (in more distant Mexico) the Aztec capital, Tenochtitlan. It was, in fact, "a city within a city".

In the absence of surviving censuses (which we know were kept by the Angkor state), it is not easy to hazard a guess about the total population of "Greater Angkor" – Groslier's figure is much too high – but Roland Fletcher (the Director of GAP) currently estimates it to have been about 700,000, making Angkor in its apogee under Jayavarman VII one of the planet's largest cities.

This great *chakravartin*, who reigned from 1181 to c.1218, was a contemporary of Genghis Khan, Saladin and Richard the Lionheart and, like them, was a great warrior in very turbulent times. In 1177 the long-standing enemies of the Khmer, the Cham kingdom of what is now Vietnam, invaded Angkor and sacked the city. Jayavarman finally defeated them in land and naval battles that are vividly portrayed on the walls of the Bayon, the temple at the centre of Angkor Thom. Early in their reigns, every major *chakravartin* felt called upon to construct: 1) a state temple, which in Jayavarman's case was the Bayon; 2) commemorative shrines to his ancestors; and 3) a *baray* (Jayavarman's is the Jayatataka, or "Sea of Victory", immediately east of Preah Khan).

Jayavarman was also a deeply religious Mahayana Buddhist, thanks (it is said) to the influence of his beautiful first wife. There were (and still are) three religions in Cambodia, and the lines between them are not always distinct. The oldest of the three is animism, melded with ancestor worship. The second is Hinduism, which has persisted not only in the rituals of Phnom Penh's Royal Palace but also in the Cambodian countryside (where the names of the old gods have been adapted to the Khmer language). Buddhism, the third religion, arrived in Cambodia at the same time as Hinduism, two millennia ago. The Mahayana Buddhism practised in Jayavarman's time was amazingly ecumenical and all-inclusive; witness the extraordinarily complex Bayon, with its Central Shrine dedicated to the Buddha, and its four-faced towers celebrating Lokeshvara – the Bodhisattva of Compassion – but with other shrines celebrating such major Hindu gods as Shiva and Vishnu. Such tolerance is seldom reciprocated by orthodox Hindus, who consider Buddhism an abominable heresy, and it is hardly surprising that after Jayavarman's death a wide and ferocious iconoclasm was visited upon Angkor's Buddhist monuments.

Under Jayavarman VII, the Khmer Empire extended over much of South-East Asia: east to the coast of Vietnam, north to Laos, north-west and west to Thailand and Burma, and south to the Malay Peninsula. Reaching to the farthest extremes of Jayavarman's realm from the capital was a highway system over which his war elephants, mounted cavalry and foot soldiers could rapidly deploy in case of invasion or insurrection. But he was an enlightened ruler, and included in his vast building programme were hospitals and rest houses.

Most notably of all, he founded within the capital three great monastic establishments, which the scholar Claude Jacques has aptly called "universities". These are: Preah Khan, built on the site of his land victory over the Cham, and dedicated to the memory of his father; Ta Prohm, built in memory of his mother; and the far simpler and less embellished Banteay Kdei. The three establishments are remarkably similar in their ground plans, and might seem to have been planned (at least in their final form) by the same anonymous architect. On my visit in 1954, when I first entered Preah Khan from the east, as all ancient and modern visitors should, I had little idea of the sophistication and complexity of its construction and iconography, other than the remarkable *apsara* lintels in the Hall of Dancers. The all-embracing ecumenism of this Mahayanist ruler can be seen in the Central Shrine, at one time containing the beautiful statue of his father as the compassionate Lokeshvara, and the complexes on the north and east, consecrated respectively to the Hindu gods Vishnu and Shiva.

But the very reverse of this humane tolerance is also visible at Preah Khan, in that every one of the several thousand Buddha images had been savagely

removed or mutilated during the post-Jayavarman iconoclasm, a chilling harbinger of what was to happen to Theravada Buddhist temples across Cambodia when Pol Pot and his Khmer Rouge came to power in 1975, the so-called "Year Zero".

I was unable to return to Angkor until 1993, when my wife, Sophie, and I arrived on the eve of the UN-supervised elections. The sound of machine-guns and mortar fire could still be heard in the distance, but it was heartening to know that even in those uncertain times non-governmental organizations of several countries were actively saving the wonders of Angkor for the

West entrance *gopura*
at Preah Khan

people of Cambodia and the world. World Monuments Fund (WMF) was
already at work stabilizing and conserving the magnificent Preah Khan, which
had virtually returned to secondary forest and had been open to looting
during those terrible decades of war and genocide. In later years I was able
again and again to visit Preah Khan and to appreciate the importance of
what WMF had accomplished, and in particular to admire their foresight in
recruiting and training Cambodian archaeologists and conservation experts
to carry on the preservation and interpretation of this beautiful monument.

Jayavarman VII would surely be pleased.

# Preah Khan: Architecture, Functions and Significance

Olivier Cunin

## Preah Khan and its associated structures

The modern name of Preah Khan, "Sacred Sword", is derived from *Nagara Jayaçri*, the ancient name of this vast complex situated in the northern area of the Angkor archaeological park. Both names refer to the reputedly miraculous weapon which was once carefully preserved in the Royal Palace of Phnom Penh. However, the original meaning of *Nagara Jayaçri* was "City of Victorious Royal Fortune". According to the Sanskrit inscription on this temple's foundation stele, discovered by Maurice Glaize in 1939 and translated by Georges Coedès, Preah Khan was linked to several settlements associated with King Jayavarman VII (1181–c.1218). These foundations are distributed around the Jayatataka, or northern *baray*, a large man-made reservoir measuring 3.6 kilometres by 940 metres, laid out to the north of the Siem Reap river and the Yasodharatataka, or eastern *baray*, founded by King Yasovarman (889–c.915). At the centre of this reservoir is a man-made island, or *mebon*, on which was erected the Neak Pean, the original name of which was Rajyasri. This *mebon* consists of several ponds situated around a sanctuary-tower. Near the northern dyke of the Jayatataka, slightly to the right of the north-south axis of the Neak Pean, the temple of Krol Kô was built. To the north-west corner of this *baray* are located two other outbuildings of Preah Khan: Prasat Prei and Banteay Prei. Delimiting the eastern end of the Jayatataka is a medium-sized complex, the Ta Som, with Preah Khan delimiting the western end.

According to the foundation stele, Preah Khan would have been situated on the site of the last battle between Jayavarman VII and the invading Chams, who were possibly associated with Khmers who had seized Angkor in 1177. This site – called "the receptacle of the blood of the enemy", and where the Cham king died – could possibly also have been the site of the earlier palace of Yasovarman II (c.1150–1165) and Tribhuvanadityavarman (c.1165–1177), prior to the Cham occupation.

OPPOSITE View along the north-south corridor (looking north) of the *stupa* in Preah Khan's Central Shrine

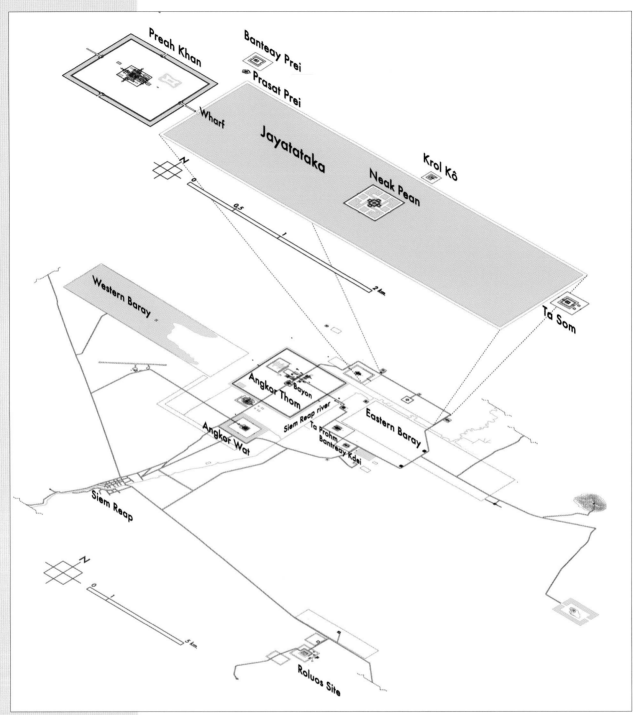

Diagram of Angkor showing
Preah Khan's relationship
to Neak Pean, Ta Som,
Prasat Prei and the Jayataka
(northern baray)

## The Preah Khan complex

The Preah Khan complex is made up of four concentric enclosures centred on
its inner sanctum. This centrifugal organization is nevertheless orientated to
the rising sun, involving an over-arching symmetry of the composition of the
monument on its east-west axis. The outer boundaries of Preah Khan are
formalized by its fourth enclosure wall, delimiting a large rectangular domain

LEFT Main pond of the Neak Pean with its sanctuary-tower on a circular islet

CENTRE General view of Prasat Prei located north of Preah Khan

BELOW Southern side of the first enclosure of Ta Som

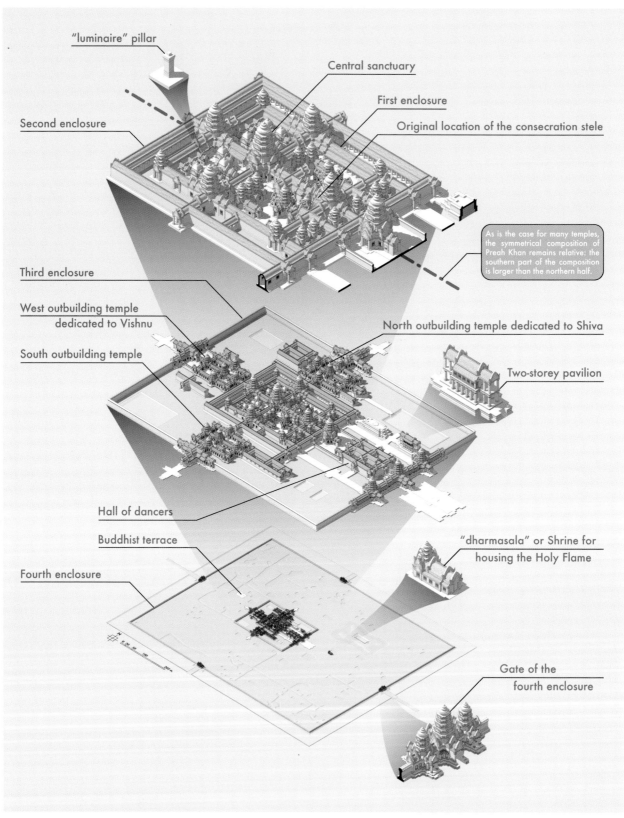

"luminaire" pillar

Central sanctuary

First enclosure

Original location of the consecration stele

Second enclosure

As is the case for many temples, the symmetrical composition of Preah Khan remains relative: the southern part of the composition is larger than the northern half.

Third enclosure

West outbuilding temple dedicated to Vishnu

North outbuilding temple dedicated to Shiva

South outbuilding temple

Two-storey pavilion

Hall of dancers

Buddhist terrace

"dharmasala" or Shrine for housing the Holy Flame

Fourth enclosure

Gate of the fourth enclosure

The Architecture of Preah Khan. As is the case for many temples, the symmetrical composition of Preah Khan remains relative: the southern part of the composition is larger than the northern half

OPPOSITE TOP *Naga* railing motif, north side of the West Causeway

OPPOSITE BELOW *Dharmasala*, to house the Holy Flame, near the east entrance to Preah Khan

of almost 53 hectares (820 x 647 metres). Six metres before this enclosure is a 47-metre-wide moat with banks built in tiers and faced with laterite. The moat is crossed by four causeway dykes leading to the monumental gates located in the fourth enclosure. The retaining walls of the causeway dykes are adorned with bas-reliefs, whereas the guard-rails are composed of giants holding the body of a polycephalous snake. Preceding the eastern and western dykes is a 95-metre-long alley flanked on either side by sandstone markers. The eastern alley ends with stairs ascending the western dyke of the Jayatataka; opposite is a jetty, from where the Neak Pean was originally accessed by boat.

The wall of the fourth enclosure was made of laterite and is over 5 metres high. Seventy-two outward-facing *garudas* in sandstone are distributed (at 50-metre intervals) along the wall. The wall is adorned with a ridge of cresting stones that contain back-to-back sandstone niches that face both towards the temple and away from it; these contained Buddha images until their removal in the thirteenth century. This outer perimeter wall of Preah Khan is traversed by four monumental gates located on the axes of distribution of the monument. The location of these gates reflects the principal axes of the temple structures, located well within the site's outer walls, and each tripartite entrance gate is capped by a false-storey tower. The central passageway below the *gopura* towers are at ground level and are wide enough for ox carts to pass. The southern and northern gates were used by both pedestrians and vehicles. Conditions along the edges of the causeways leading to the eastern and western entrances would have hindered vehicular access.

A forest presently covers the space between the fourth and the third

enclosure walls delimiting the religious complex. These large quadrants probably contained ensembles of wooden constructions used by monks and civil
servants associated with the temple's operation and its outbuildings. According to the temple's consecration stele, it seems that Preah Khan was a city that
contained an active and extensive centre of Buddhist learning. Only a few
remains have been recovered of the perishable monastic structures that
existed in the ordinary residential quadrants of Preah Khan. In the north-east
quadrant there remains a *dharmasala*, the structure that housed the Holy
Flame, to the north of which lies a large rectangular pond (53 x 24 metres)
surrounded by a moat. In the north-west quadrant a Buddhist terrace was
erected some two centuries after Preah Khan was founded.

All the architecture within the three inner walls of Preah Khan is positioned in relation to the temple's central axes, which provide access to the
site's principal Central Sanctuary-tower. The third enclosure wall delimits a
rectangle of around 217 x 162 metres. It consists of a laterite wall more than
2 metres high and is traversed on the cardinal points by an entrance pavilion
preceded by a cruciform causeway. Only the most important entrance
pavilion – the eastern – was surmounted by a prominent false-storey tower.
The first and second enclosures of the temple and several buildings are
located inside this area, with the density of buildings increasing in relation to
the proximity to Preah Khan's inner sanctum.

The space between the third and second enclosures of Preah Khan contains five ponds, with the north-eastern one, measuring 51 x 20 metres, having
embankments faced with laterite layers. To the south of this pond are located
two constructions connected by a causeway made of sandstone. The walls of

the base of the western building are faced with laterite, and its upper platform may have supported a wooden construction. The symmetrical construction opposite has an unusual form in Khmer architecture: a pavilion supported by columns, which was entirely restored using the anastylosis technique (which entailed re-erecting collapsed building elements). Only three such ancient Khmer two-storey constructions in sandstone are known. The two others, located in Ta Prohm and Banteay Kdei, are badly damaged and were built with pillars instead of columns. To the south of these two buildings, located on the main axis of the temple, is a large cruciform construction with four small inner courtyards: the Hall of Dancers. The name comes from the *apsara* friezes carved above the lintels of the inner doors. Two buildings known as "libraries" are constructed adjacent to the western side of the Hall of Dancers, as are two laterite walls connecting with the second enclosure that form a courtyard where a *prasat*, or sanctuary-tower, was erected. Finally, three religious complexes housing sizeable stone shrines occupy the north, west and south parts between the temple's third and second enclosures. The galleries of these complexes contain shrines (central tower and tower pavilions) and "library" structures. Their Central Sanctuaries are connected to the galleries by a hypostyle hall on the east-west axis. Noticeable in the west *gopura* towers of the western religious complex are some remnants of painted finishes that are suggestive of the appearance and aesthetics of both the interiors and the exteriors of many other Khmer royal or religious works of architecture.

The second enclosure is situated only 5.5 metres from the temple's first, innermost enclosure wall and delimits a courtyard of approximately 77 x 66 metres. This enclosure is mainly constructed in laterite and forms a perimeter gallery with a side-nave opening inwards. The eastern space between the first two enclosures is occupied by six sanctuary-towers with scant remains of décor and evidence that some surfaces were unfinished.

This central architectural feature of Preah Khan is surrounded by its own border, the first enclosure, which contains an area of approximately 52 x 41 metres. Pavilions capped with false-storey towers mark the cardinal points at the corners of this enclosure. The Central Sanctuary of Preah Khan, around which the entire compositional arrangement is organized, does not mark the geometrical centre of the first enclosure. The central tower shrine follows a square stepped plan preceded by antechambers at its cardinal points and off-centred to the west, owing to the presence of a *mandapa*, or hypostyle hall. The other antechambers are linked to north, west and south axial towers in the first enclosure by colonnaded galleries consisting of central, high-ceilinged corridors flanked by aisles. The (subsequently formed) two eastern courtyards within the first enclosure wall are occupied respectively by four *prasats* of different sizes to the north and by five to the south. Some of them are preceded by a *mandapa* or linked to the first gallery by a connecting construction. Each of the two western courtyards contains seven sandstone shrines, the *cella* (principal chamber) of each having once contained a deity. Many of them are integrated into the gallery of the first enclosure or in the north and south connecting galleries of the Central Sanctuary. Two pillars, called *luminaires*, further define these two courtyards.

## The functions of Preah Khan

As with the other monuments in the Bayon style, Preah Khan was a Mahayana ("Great Vehicle") Buddhist foundation. It was dedicated simultaneously to Lokeshvara (Avalokitesvara), the Bodhisattva of Compassion, and to Dharanindravarman, the father of Jayavarman VII. The raising of Buddhism to the rank of state cult during the reign of Jayavarman VII did not signal the disappearance of the old Hindu state cults in the royal foundations. Actually, as at the Bayon and probably also Banteay Chhmar, Preah Khan was a temple dedicated to Vishnu. The Hindu iconography of these two secondary religious complexes was nevertheless constrained by Buddhist iconography. This apparent syncretism in the architectural and iconographic programme of Preah Khan displays the great religious tolerance of the era of Jayavarman VII.

The religious practices at Preah Khan and the other Bayon-style monuments may not have been very different from those of the Hindu temples of the preceding reigns. Indeed, in spite of their Buddhist persuasion, the monuments of Jayavarman VII do not show any major typological evolution among the structures that comprise them. Thus, we find again the sanctuary-towers (*prasats*), the buildings today called "libraries" and the gallery-enclosures that had been formalized in the course of the eleventh century. The Hall of Dancers differs little from the "cruciform galleries" of Angkor Wat and Beng Mealea, dating to the first half of the twelfth century. Only the "two-storey pavilion" constitutes an innovation in the vocabulary of Angkorian architecture. Indeed,

Defaced bas reliefs of Buddha images showing evidence of iconoclasm during the 13th century, in Preah Khan's Central Sanctuary

the cult areas of Jayavarman VII's complexes were not adapted to accommodate a large number of devotees, unlike the Gothic cathedrals built in Europe during the same period.

Fundamentally theatrical and imprinted with a strong religious symbolism, Khmer stone architecture was made to be seen from the outside. The corbelling technique used for the superstructures of the *prasats* and buildings that could serve as sanctuaries, such as the "libraries", allowed only a small space, which was largely occupied by the divine images (and their pedestals) which were placed inside them. Only one or two functionaries could have taken their place in front of the divinity to carry out their prescribed rituals at certain times of the day (ablution, offerings of food or of dance). The rest of the time these sanctuaries were closed by wooden double-doors installed at their openings. The Buddhist complexes of Jayavarman VII would have been spaces that were as highly hierarchical as the Hindu temples of his predecessors. The closer one got to the Holy of Holies, the more access was reserved for the monastic community and the élite of the Khmer society.

## Preah Khan's architectural history

As for all buildings erected by Jayavarman VII, the Preah Khan complex and associated structures were built in several phases. There were five main phases of architectural development in the case of Preah Khan, all associated with the

reign of Jayavarman VII and later his direct heir, Indravarman II (c.1218–1270). In the thirteenth century the essential Buddhist iconography of the monuments of the Bayon style located in Angkor was partially destroyed or modified when (Hindu) Shivaism briefly seized power again in Angkor. This major change in religious preference is usually associated with the reign of Jayavarman VIII (1270–1295). It was probably politically motivated and explains the destruction of the external décor of the Central Sanctuary of Ta Prohm, Preah Khan and the Bayon. These three temples were a representation of the scale of Angkor's Buddhist trinity (Prajnaparamita, Avalokitesvara and Buddha) and of the family trinity (mother, father and son) of Jayavarman VII.

Towards the end of the Angkorian era the predominant religion became once again Theravada Buddhism, "the doctrine of the elders", which is the main form of the religion practised today in Cambodia. It was probably during this period that the Buddhist terrace of the north-west quadrant of the fourth enclosure of the monument was built. A few changes to the iconography also took place at this time. The abandonment of Angkor in the fifteenth century did not end religious practices in Preah Khan. Around the sixteenth century a masonry *stupa* was erected in the inner sanctum at the location where, before Angkor's iconoclast turmoil, the statue of Avalokitesvara may have stood.

Unlike at Ta Prohm, Banteay Kdei and Ta Som, the surrounding walls that formalized the vast domain of Preah Khan were erected during the history of the site. Decorative elements of monumental gates and of wall crests indicate that the surrounding wall was built during the third phase of the construction of the temple. It is nevertheless more likely that the moats were excavated during the first construction phase. The earth removed during moat excavations was probably used to raise central portions of the site for proper drainage before the first phase of construction.

This first phase consisted of building the primary religious area of Preah Khan, starting with the Central Sanctuary. This included the site's first and third enclosure walls and the northern, western and southern building complexes. A single tower was erected in a corresponding location to the west in this first phase. This initial phase of construction at Preah Khan represents a major development in the extensive architectural programme of Jayavarman VII. It is at Preah Khan that the typology of the great temples in the Bayon style was formalized.

Four typologies may have existed at the beginning of the reign of Jayavarman VII, each corresponding to a hierarchical class of monuments. The use of each model depended on the value suggested by the location and function of the site, thus constituting a network of foundations to administer the kingdom. The novelty of Preah Khan compared with its predecessor, Ta Prohm, is in the formalization of associated building complexes, forming sanctuaries that are almost equidistant from the main sanctuary. The eventual general composition refers to the Buddhist *mandala*, an idiom later represented by the upper platform of the Bayon, and which informed the large expansion programme of Banteay Chhmar, a major temple of Jayavarman VII located in north-west Cambodia, near the Thai border.

OPPOSITE Masonry *stupa* erected in the Central Sanctuary, c.16th century

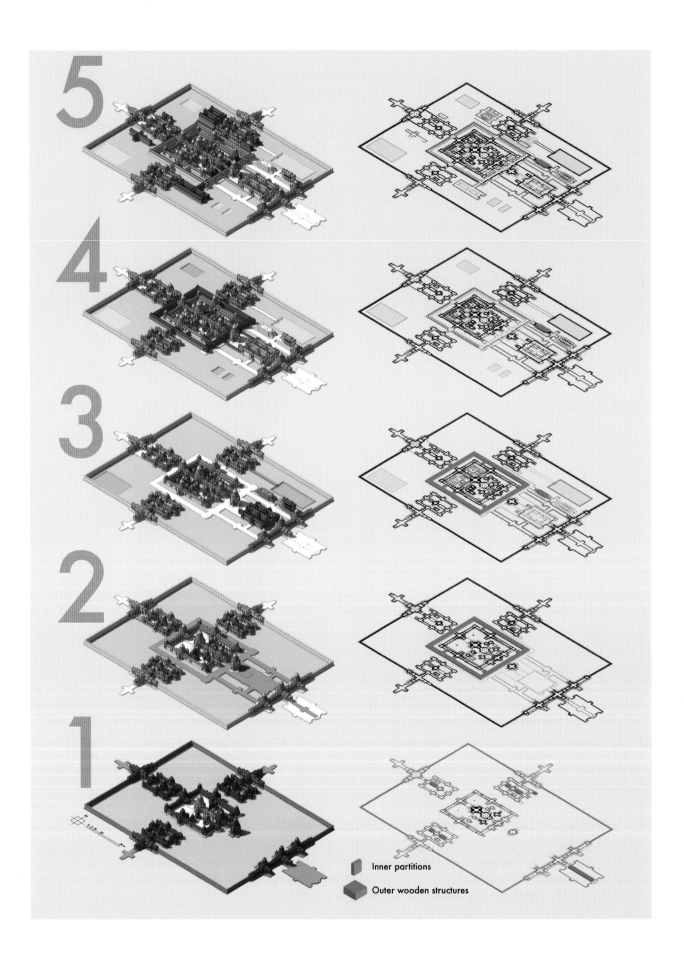

**5**

**4**

**3**

**2**

**1**

Inner partitions

Outer wooden structures

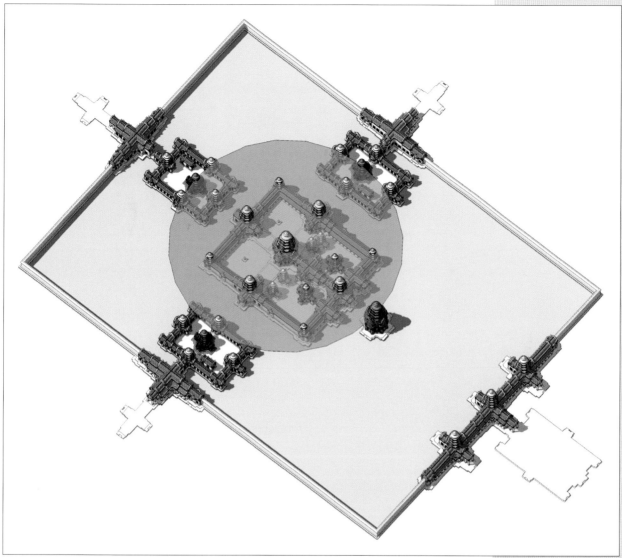

OPPOSITE Relative chronology of the construction phases of Preah Khan. Phases 1–3 were completed by 1192 or 1193; phases 4 and 5, c.1218 to 1270

ABOVE Depiction of the inital construction phase of the basic components of Preah Khan, showing the spatial distribution of sanctuary-towers

The scope of the architectural programme of Jayavarman VII may have been one of the reasons for the systematic use of wooden structures in less valuable areas during the early phases of Preah Khan's construction. Thus the second enclosure at the site, and some connecting passageways between the sanctuary-towers, were constructed in wood and later rebuilt in a similar style in stone. This system of replacing wooden forms with more durable materials is the main explanation for the complexity of the history of Bayon-style monuments. Yet the use of wooden walls forming Preah Khan's inner three enclosure-galleries distinguishes the temple from other temples in the Bayon style. At Preah Khan the first enclosure had wooden partitions, and this system of division was carried out when wooden partitions were replaced with stone ones at the second enclosure of the temple during the fourth phase of construction. The main function of this gallery was not ambulatory but rather to accommodate a series of integral open rooms where a number of the site's 430 secondary divinities that are mentioned on the monument's stele may have been placed.

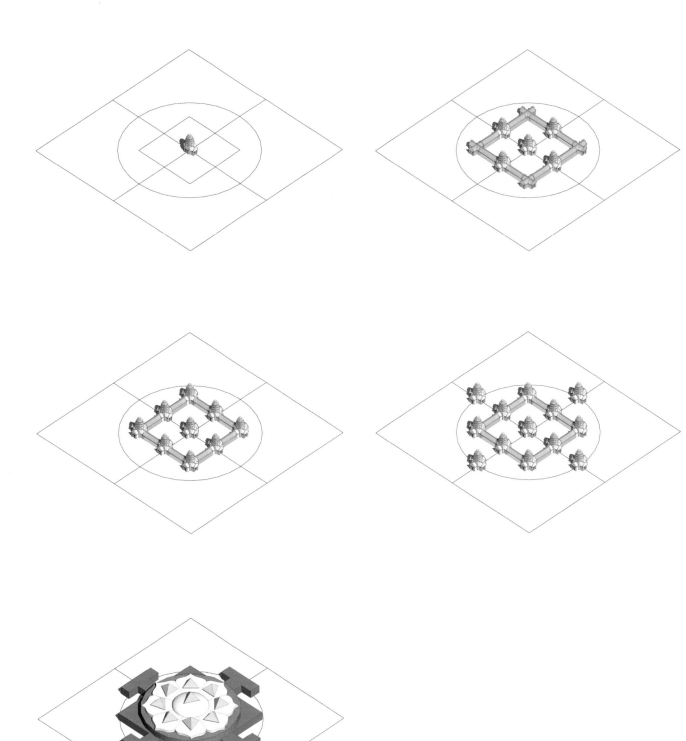

Schematic drawings showing (a) the first type of Bayon-style temple consisting of one *prasat*, e.g. Prasat Prei (b) the second type, consisting of a principal central *prasat*, further defined by four *prasats* located at the cardinal points (north, east, south, west), e.g. Ta Som, Banteay Prei (c) the third type, composed of one *prasat* delimited with eight *prasats* located on the cardinal and intercardinal points, e.g. Wat Nokor, Banteay Kdei once transformed (d) the fourth type, composed of one *prasat* delimited with eight *prasats* located on the cardinal and intercardinal points, the latter delimited by four *prasats* located on the cardinal points, e.g. Ta Prohm, Preah Khan, Banteay Chhmar and Bayon. The spatial distribution of the prasats at Preah Khan is based on the Buddhist *mandala*

It is difficult to establish a time-frame for each phase of construction at
Preah Khan. Nevertheless, a comparison between the spatial distribution of
the temple's divine population (complete images of the deity, usually in sandstone or bronze) cited on the temple's stele, and the location and information
given in small inscriptions in Khmer elsewhere, suggests that the third construction phase was already complete by 1192 or 1193 – the date given for the
consecration of the monument stele.

Several architectural precedents were established during the first five
phases of construction of Preah Khan that served as the basis for further developments at the Bayon and Banteay Chhmar, such as the spatial distribution
of the *prasats* based on the Buddhist *mandala* and the style of architectural
décor (roof ridges, false windows etc.) and of ornamental décor (door jamb
motifs, *devatas* and so on). However, noticeable by its absence at Preah Khan
is one motif that symbolizes practically all of Jayavarman VII's largest monastic complexes: the Face Towers. Although this emblematic symbol appears at
the Bayon, on the five monumental gateways to Angkor Thom, Ta Prohm,
Banteay Kdei, Ta Som, Banteay Chhmar and at Preah Khan of Kampong Svay,
there is no explanation as to why this "signature" element is not present at
Preah Khan. Was the Face Tower motif developed after the towers of Preah
Khan were erected? Yet the Face Tower motif was already in existence during
the last construction phase of Preah Khan. The omission looks deliberate, so
perhaps it was related to the motif's problematic symbolism. This is one of
the numerous riddles posed by Preah Khan that remains to be solved, and
another distinguishing feature of this special site.

35

# The Preah Khan Stele

Claude Jacques

The external appearance of the dedication stele of Preah Khan is similar to that of steles erected by King Jayavarman VII in other temples, including Ta Prohm, Banteay Chhmar and Prasat Chrungs (located at the four corners of Angkor Thom). On a very fine sandstone pillar measuring 0.60 x 2.2 metres, long poems composed in Sanskrit were carved, consisting of a total of 179 stanzas – more than 700 alexandrines (iambic hexameters) – almost all of which are still legible. This poem is one of the most valuable epigraphic monuments of the ancient Khmer civilization, providing a wealth of concrete information.

It begins with a short tribute to divinities and then continues by recalling the genealogy of King Jayavarman VII, citing his distinguished ancestors. It is a long genealogy, which acknowledges that the king's rights to the throne were not obvious. Next is a rare but relatively short eulogy of the king (in 13 stanzas). The following stanza refers to the foundation date of the temple of Preah Khan and its main divinities as being in either 1192 or 1193. (The official foundation date of such temples is the point when the base and the pedestal of the divinity are built, which means that the construction of Preah Kahn was actually completed later.) As it is believed that the poem was composed when the original plan of the temple was completed, one can infer that the stele was engraved in the late twelfth century, at the earliest. This is useful for the history of the temple, since it is well known that Preah Khan was extended or modified in the thirteenth century and probably again during the following century or centuries. The stele therefore allows us to distinguish between the original design and what was built later.

After discussing the date of the foundation of the temple, the poem describes royal achievements, in two sections: one section is about the temple of Preah Khan and its outbuildings, and the other is about the overall achievements of the king. The two sections are similar in structure. The first part gives an inventory of all the divinities located in the temple, and then details the daily quantity of rice and other ingredients to feed them, and ends by

OPPOSITE The Preah Khan
dedication stele in situ, 1996

quoting the annual quantity consumed. The king and landlords of the villages provided all these ingredients. A list of miscellaneous products and items necessary for the cult follows. The second part provides a list with figures of the materials required for several types of construction at Preah Khan, similar to the calculations a quantity surveyor would put together.

To interpret these lists and figures accurately is no simple task, although there is a pleasing wealth of concrete information about the temple and its daily life, even if the details contain some surprising – at times, even disconcerting – information which raises further problems of interpretation. For instance, the lines that describe the Preah Khan temple and its associated structures as housing 515 divinities are surprising. With this number in a temple the size of Preah Khan, it is hard to imagine how these gods would have been grouped. Would they have been arranged next to each other, perhaps along each of the temple's many galleries? Another surprising statistic is the stated volume of rice offered to these divinities – on average more than four tons per day – but this would have been required not only for the gods but also for priests and their families, and probably also for worshippers attending services.

The second part of the inscription detailing royal achievements comprises a list of associated temples in the region, including Wat Nokor in Kampong Cham and Banteay Chhmar – on a site called Ksac – near the present Thai border, 25 sanctuaries dedicated to the rather mysterious Jayabuddha-mahânâtha ("Buddha Vanquisher and Great Protector") and 121 temples dedicated to the Holy Flame, built along the roads.

The poem continues by briefly describing the temple's annual ceremony, to which Buddha and the main gods of the empire – the gods of Wat Nokor, Ta Prohm, Banteay Chhmar and Phimai, among others (which were cited earlier in the description of the foundation of Preah Khan) – were invited as guests. A remarkable absentee from the list of gods mentioned on the Preah Khan stele is the Buddha of the Bayon, which raises questions about the date of its consecration. This section ends with another list of offerings presented by the king for this occasion.

The poem concludes with 11 long stanzas in which the king makes a plea to his successors to protect his religious works. Some of these stanzas are fine poetry, which also provide additional details. Thus we learn that the site of Neak Pean, dedicated to Shiva by Jayavarman VII before being converted strictly to Buddhism, was delimited only by the large, central pond, so the additional four smaller ponds centred on the site's cardinal points were built later. The last two stanzas in this part indicate that, to provide the rice required to support Preah Khan and its associated sanctuaries, 306,372 people living in 13,500 villages worked to yield the annual equivalent of 24,000 tons of white rice. This is some of the best evidence to date of the major economic role played by Angkor's great temples.

The last stanza of the Preah Khan stele provides evidence of the culture of the royal family by revealing that the poem is the work of Prince Vīrakumāra, a son of Jayavarman VII, and of one of his queens, named Rājendradevī.

# Imagery, Symbolism and Mythology at Preah Khan

Dawn F. Rooney

Imagery at the monastic complex of Preah Khan is the quintessential example of the amalgamation of beliefs that existed during the reign of Jayavarman VII (1181–c.1218). A harmonious admixture of sculpture culled from Buddhist and Hindu mythology is richly carved in sandstone and adorns walls, lintels, pediments, pilasters and door jambs. Enlightened beings in Mahayana Buddhism preside over the central complex, while two Hindu gods – Vishnu and Shiva – are honoured in shrines in the western and northern sectors of the temple. The southern complex is dedicated to the king's uncle, and Jayavarman VII built Preah Khan to honour his father, continuing the long, indigenous tradition of ancestor worship.

The sculpture was made to glorify the temple, which was an earthly replica of the cosmic world. It includes free-standing images in the round and carvings in high relief. Some are narratives from well-known episodes in mythology while others, such as heavenly nymphs, embellish the temple with their beauty. Sculpture of the period tends towards realism, with a more human quality than in earlier works, in response to a shift from Hinduism to Mahayana Buddhism, the state religion of the king. Typical facial features – a broad forehead, downcast eyes and the hint of an enigmatic smile – suggest a mystical yet compassionate nature, characteristics that convey the spiritual and artistic ideal of the late twelfth and early thirteenth centuries.

A majestic processional way flanked by rectangular stone *bornes* (pillars resembling lanterns) is unique to Preah Khan and signals the richness of sculpture inside the temple. Each lantern is 91 centimetres high, with a round finial at the top. A mythical animal with a human torso, the legs of Garuda ("guardian birdman") and the face of a lion stands at the base on four sides with arms raised, as though supporting it with his might. The niches at the top originally housed seated Buddhas, but nearly all Buddhist imagery was destroyed, defaced or altered during the reign of a subsequent king in the thirteenth century who made a concerted effort to transform Preah Khan into a Hindu temple. Many meditating Buddha images were carved into seated

OPPOSITE One of a pair of *devatas* (female divinities) adorning both sides of a niche, north-west quadrant of Preah Khan

40

Hindu ascetics by changing the position of the legs and arms, altering the facial expression and adding a goatee.

The abundance of *naga* (serpent) symbolism at Preah Khan is not surprising, as the Khmers claim their descent from the union of a foreigner with a daughter of the *naga* king. Equally at home in Buddhist and Hindu mythology, *nagas* live underground at the bottom of watery places in palaces studded with pearls and precious gems. They symbolize the life force and wield universal power as keepers of life-giving energy and guardians of the sea's wealth.

A dramatic example of the *naga* theme in Khmer art appears on the sandstone-paved causeway that crosses the moat leading to the outer enclosure of the temple. Massive sculptures of *devas* (gods) and *asuras* (demons), 54 on each side, flank the causeway. They hold the scaly body of the *naga* Vasuki, who spreads his multiple heads at one end and entwines his upraised tail at the other, forming a balustrade along the causeway. Preah Khan is the only temple at Angkor where this ensemble appears at all four entrances. Scholars debate the meaning of the figures. The most widespread explanation is that they represent the Churning of the Ocean of Milk, a Hindu myth in the *Bhagavatapurana*. Vasuki's body is the rope, and the gods and demons pull and push in a churning action, attempting to extract the elixir of immortality.

Whenever the world is threatened by evil, Vishnu, the preserver, descends to earth in one of his many forms and tries to restore balance between the dual forces. In this episode he appears as a tortoise and lends his hard-shelled back for the pivot of the churning. Other interpretations of the meaning of the figures include the idea that, as they total the sacred number of 108, they may be guardians of the temple and they perhaps form a bridge represented by a rainbow where one crosses over from the human world to that of the gods.

Further protection of Preah Khan is garnered by 72 astonishing images (35 metres apart) of the mythical bird Garuda standing sentinel against the outer enclosure wall. Garuda's appearance is formidable. Feathers cover his human torso and he has the wings and talons of an eagle, a broad, hooked beak and bulging eyes. The *naga* is his arch-enemy. The story of their contempt for each other unfolds in the *Mahabharata*, one of the great Indian epics. Garuda's aunt enslaved his mother but promised her freedom if Garuda stole the elixir of immortality. So Garuda flew to the heaven of Indra (god of the sky) and trounced the two huge serpents that guarded the elixir by blowing dust into their eyes. The *garudas* at Preah Khan enact this heroic myth by trampling the *nagas* with their talons and holding the *nagas'* tails aloft with raised arms. The *nagas'* multiple heads unfurl beside the legs of the *garudas*. Vishnu was so impressed with Garuda's defeat of the serpents that he assigned him to be his vehicle and used him to fly through the universe at a speed faster than lightning. World Monuments Fund has adopted the *garuda* as the protector of Preah Khan.

Most of the free-standing sculpture in the round that once adorned the temple is either in a museum collection or has been stolen. A pair of colossal *dvarapalas* ("guardians of the gate"), however, remain *in situ* and stand with a commanding presence at the entrance to the third enclosure. As bearers of the duality of good and evil, the *dvarapalas* have the task of keeping bad spirits out and admitting the benevolent. Even though the heads and attributes of these figures are missing, one can glean their personae from examples carved on door jambs inside the temple. The *dvarapala* on the right wears a kind expression and holds a trident; the one on the left bears a fierce expression, with bulging eyes, and wields a club. Some of the characteristics of thirteenth-century male sculpture can be seen in the legs of the *dvarapalas*, which are particularly thick in proportion to the torso, and in the well-defined kneecaps and short garment.

A superb pediment inside the temple depicts a variation on the Hindu myth recalling the birth of Brahma. In the original story Vishnu is recumbent on the body of the serpent Ananta (meaning "infinite"), and floats on the ocean of eternal life in a cosmic sleep. The Hindu god Brahma, the creator, emerges seated in a lotus bloom as its stem rises from Vishnu's navel. Brahma then sets a new creation in motion, and thus the endless cycle of rebirth continues. In the pediment here, Brahma's birth is only implied, indicated by a lotus stem with three budding branches. And the serpent assumes a dragon-like appearance, with short legs, an elongated body, a lion's head and mane, an upturned snout and a goatee. Vishnu's consort massages his feet.

A powerful narrative scene depicts the Hindu god Shiva, creator and destroyer of the universe, in his manifestation as Nataraja ("the Lord of the Dance"). He dances energetically, with his 10 arms vibrating wildly as he spins and whirls through time and space in a performance proclaiming victory over evil. The rhythmic dance encapsulates the cosmic cycle of generation and destruction.

Ethereal *devatas* (female divinities) standing in niches on the walls, pillars and corners epitomize a transcendent beauty that resonated with the

Dreaming Vishnu figure, fronton detail, north-west quadrant of Preah Khan

Khmer aesthetic taste of the period. One *devata* holds a lotus stem in the hand of her raised arm (see page 41). Her sarong is decorated with a floral pattern suggesting a sumptuous fabric like silk. The light incising of the garment reflects a progressive trend towards simplicity in the sculpture of the thirteenth century. Her headdress (which in some examples is framed by a delicate halo) tapers to a pinnacle and she is richly adorned with anklets, bracelets, armlets and a jewel-encrusted belt.

The Hall of Dancers at the east of the temple derives its name from the

RIGHT Shiva in his manifestation as Nataraja, fronton detail, western Vishnu complex at Preah Khan

BELOW Detail of *apsaras*, bas relief in east-facing inner lintel, west entrance of the Hall of Dancers

magnificent lintels carved with a bevy of *apsaras* (celestial dancers), who some believe were born of the Churning of the Ocean of Milk. They reside in celestial mansions in Indra's realm. The seductive powers of the ever-youthful *apsaras* are boundless, particularly over men, and they are the consummate dispensers of sensual delight. The largest lintel found at Angkor so far is at the Hall of Dancers at Preah Khan (west face). Fourteen supple *apsaras* in a sinuous dance posture span its width. They are poised on the toes of one foot, with the other leg flexed in the opposite direction and both arms raised, with hands bent backwards. They wear short skirts held in place by belts with pendants hanging from them, elaborate tiaras inlaid with precious gems, and long, dangling earrings. A jasmine garland is loosely draped around the neck of the central figure. The *apsaras* dance in unison, surely to the rhythmic cadence of musical accompaniment.

Image in bronze of the Buddhistic triad in the Bayon style, Jayavarman VII period

A triad of three divine beings in one spirit, cast in bronze and now in the National Museum of Cambodia, manifests the symbiotic nature of imagery at Preah Khan. Many more such triads (either in bronze or stone) must have existed, as the three beings are invoked at the beginning of most of Jayavarman VII's inscriptions. The Buddha, seated in meditation on an open lotus and protected by the *naga*, is the central figure in the triad. He holds a medicine jar identifying him as the Buddha of healing. The posture depicts an episode that took place after Prince Siddhartha attained enlightenment at Bodhgaya in India. While the Buddha was meditating, a torrential storm began to brew, unbeknown to him. Muchalinda, the *naga* king, detected the storm, rose from the murky waters and coiled his body three times to raise the Buddha off the ground. Then he fanned his seven heads like an umbrella to shelter the Buddha from the storm. For the Khmers, the theme of the Buddha meditating on a *naga* harked back to the origin of their dynasty and the legendary ancestor who married a *naga* princess.

Lokeshvara ("the Lord of the World"), standing to the Buddha's right, is a Bodhisattva and a form of Avalokitesvara ("the Lord who Looks Down with Compassion"), who elected to stay on earth to help mankind achieve enlightenment rather than become a Buddha. Amitabha Jina, a miniature meditating Buddha who presides over the western paradise, appears in the chignon of Lokeshvara and is his distinguishing characteristic. He is usually depicted with four arms holding a rosary, a book, a flask and a lotus bud. As the protector, healer and helper of all mankind, Lokeshvara was a model for the king. Thus Jayavarman VII placed an image of him in the Central Sanctuary of Preah Khan and dedicated the temple to Lokeshvara in honour of his father.

Prajnaparamita ("the Perfection of Wisdom"), the third member of the triad, stands to the Buddha's left. She is the feminine personification and a mother goddess figure. She holds a lotus bud and sometimes a book. The king dedicated the temple of Ta Prohm to Prajnaparamita in honour of his mother.

The sculpture embellishing the celestial abode of Preah Khan built by Jayavarman VII in the late twelfth century is imbued with a richness that celebrates his belief in Mahayana Buddhism and the embodiment of wisdom and compassion, as seen in his homage to the Buddhist triad.

# A Temple Revealed

Christophe Pottier

We meet Yem Ek in the afternoon of 19 May 2009, in the village of Nokor Krav, located 2 kilometres to the west of Preah Khan. Also called Ta Ek ("Ek the Old"), he is completing a *kanchoeu*, one of the traditional round baskets with a square base which, coated with a vegetal layer, serves as a bucket. Now 69, Ta Ek seldom goes to tend the fields any more. He stays at home, sitting cross-legged on a bench, shaded by a thatched hut that also houses chickens and cattle. His days are now spent in handicrafts.

Calm, uncomplaining and in matter-of-fact fashion, Ta Ek has been relating the ups and downs of life in the village and of the Preah Khan region since the invasion of Angkor on 5 June 1970 by the Khmer Rouge and their Viet Cong allies. Fleeing the bombardments of Lon Nol's artillery, thousands of villagers took refuge in the galleries of Angkor Wat and the Bayon. Others, like Ta Ek, took shelter a few kilometres further north. Then, despite their status as "old people", they were forcefully and repeatedly displaced to other, more remote locations during the Khmer Rouge era.

They finally returned to Nokor Krav in 1979, still subject to intermittent fighting between the Khmer Rouge guerrillas and the Vietnamese troops positioned at one end of the village, on the northern gate of Angkor Thom. The Khmer Rouge regularly invaded the area, causing further displacements. There were bombings and artillery fire, and mines and other types of ordinance were laid anywhere and everywhere, even in the tilled rice fields.

Then, during the early 1990s, more secure conditions prevailed, and the restoration sites were reopened. In 1992, Ta Ek was hired by the École Française d'Extrême-Orient (EFEO) to work on the Terrace of the Leper King, before making way for his son Yem Khon. The latter joins us in the house after changing from the uniform of the World Monuments Fund (WMF) – his present-day employer at the Bakheng Temple – to put on the more comfortable *krama* (a Cambodian scarf).

For the Yem and several other families of the Nokor Krav village, the restoration of Angkor has become a kind of family tradition. Ta Ek is one of a

OPPOSITE The Two-Storey Pavilion at Preah Khan prior to removal of vegetation, 1940

ABOVE Khmer worker Ta Ek in 1955 hoisting stone at Preah Khan's principal east entrance *gopura* under direction of the EFEO

OPPOSITE The Two-Storey Pavilion during reconstruction by the EFEO using the anastylosis process, 1952

handful of surviving workers who have dedicated a large part of their lives to the cleaning and restoration of the Angkorian monuments. Ta Ek smiles, remembering how, at the age of only 15, he was hired by the Angkor Conservation organization. Since at that time the required minimum age was 18, Corporal Crom – who had hired him, after taking a cut in his salary – ordered Ta Ek to hide in the forest every time the *barang* (the French Curator) visited the site. So this boy from Nokor Krav was only 15 when he first set foot in an Angkorian temple, which happened to be Preah Khan. Before this, young Yem Ek was too busy looking after cattle, and had been to Angkor Wat only to attend the *chaul chram* (Khmer New Year) ceremonies.

In Preah Khan he took part in the restoration of the northern *gopura* of the third enclosure and in the clearing of the courtyard of the secondary north sanctuary; until he reached 18 he played hide-and-seek with the Curator, Jean Laur. Then, at the age of 25 – following a brief stint "wearing the robe" at the northern monastery of Angkor Wat – he married and joined his wife (one of the seven women employed at Angkor Conservation) working at the south gate of Angkor Thom, and finally at the Terrace of the Leper King until 1970. From these years spent with Angkor Conservation, during which he was supervised by a succession of corporals and French officials (who were fore-

men rather than "great curators"), Ta Ek remembers good pay and "pleasant" work – although he admits it was as tiring as tending rice fields.

The tasks remembered by Ta Ek give a concrete account of the nature of works carried out by Angkor Conservation: building and then dismantling scaffolding made of wood, bamboo and vines, searching for missing blocks of stone, carrying and hoisting them. But these memories do not give a complete picture of the scope and activities of this institution, which was created in 1907 – the date when Siem Reap was reunited with the Kingdom of Cambodia, and when the EFEO was entrusted with the management of the Angkor site. Although Ta Ek first saw Preah Khan in 1955, he had arrived at the completion of an endeavour started more than 30 years earlier.

Daily excavation logs, monthly reports and thousands of drawings and pictures left by the successive curators provide a wealth of detailed documentation of the work carried out at Preah Khan. Looking at their documents, one realizes the part they played in facilitating visits to a site now famous for its spectacular axial perspectives. These are the results of the long cleaning works started by Henri Marchal in 1927 on the main east-west axis. These began at the eastern end, at the jetty overlooking the Jayatataka (the northern *baray* of the Neak Pean), then continued west in the direction of the central tower, which was finally reached in 1940 by Maurice Glaize. By 1946 the east-west axis had been completely cleared; in 1957 the clearing of the north-south axis was mostly completed by Jean Laur.

So for 30 years Preah Khan had been a continuously worked site, affected only by twentieth-century historical events, such as the Depression of 1932–39, the imprisonment of the French Curator (George Groslier) in 1945 during the Japanese occupation, and the subsequent troubled period of the Issarak guerrillas from 1946–49. All of these events interrupted this work. Preah Khan is certainly a good illustration of the difficulties accompanying the apparently straightforward clearing of the Angkor temples, buried deep in the forest. While cleaning of the major temples of Angkor Wat and the Bayon was begun in 1908, it was completed at the other main temples only in the late 1950s, at a time when Angkor Conservation fell under the jurisdiction of the newly independent government of Angkor.

The nature of this work also testifies to the evolution of the restoration techniques applied to the entire site of Angkor. Early on, the technique adopted by Marchal utilized the fabrication of concrete props – the famous "jambettes Marchal" – along with partial reinforcement works. These reassemblies were sometimes colossal, such as the reconstruction of the superstructures of the eastern *gopuras* of the third and fourth enclosure, or the re-setting of the bas-relief stones cladding both sides of the eastern causeway and of the *naga* railings on top.

In 1930, inspired by the reconstruction method employed by the Dutch at Borobudur in Java, Marchal introduced to Angkor the reconstruction technique called "anastylosis". This method consists of rebuilding a dilapidated monument based on the identification of the exact origin of each of its constituent stones. At Preah Khan, at the Two-Storey Pavilion, Marchal trained Corporal Svai and his team for three months, then sent them to the rebuilding of Banteay Srei, leaving the Two-Storey Pavilion with only the columns standing – an anastylosis he finally resumed and completed 22 years later (see page 53).

Marchal noted that "the era of Jayavarman VII", a time when building was carried out quickly and carelessly, "ought to be the last to be selected" for trying the anastylosis technique introduced to the region by the Dutch (Angkor Conservation report, November 1930). Obviously Marchal was wrong: he failed to anticipate the success of anastylosis in Angkor, and in particular at Preah Kahn, where his successors Glaize and Laur used the technique extensively, reconstructing several structures, principally on the main axis and in the first enclosure of the Central Sanctuary.

The scope of the reconstruction carried out in Preah Khan reflected the paradoxical position of this temple among the complex of Angkorian monuments. It was categorically included among the other great temples of Jayavarman VII, although not given high priority by Angkor's first archaeologists, who assigned this status largely to the few "temple-mountain" or pyramid forms. Nevertheless, as clearing progressed, and with an increasing awareness that this complex also included the Jayatataka and neighbouring associated temples, it was realized that the size and architectural qualities of Preah Khan, as a key feature in a huge architectural complex, distinguished it

from the others, especially from the privileged Ta Prohm (which had been
cleared by 1920).

From that time onwards Preah Khan illustrated the long search for a com-
promise – instead of a solution – to the reconciliation of two opposites by
complementary conservation schemes that appeared early on at Angkor Conservation. The first advocated the restoration and preservation of major,
significant monuments, eradicating the forest, as was the case at the Bayon.
The second conversely aimed to keep some sites, in the words of Maurice
Glaize, "in the natural condition which had greatly impressed the first explor-
ers". Glaize was a great advocate of the first approach, but admitted that the
second showed "in comparison the importance of the effort [to] safeguard
old stones".

George Groslier, who was more sensitive to the poetry of ruins buried
under the forest, recalled the condition of Preah Khan before it was cleared.
He described Preah Khan as:

Watercolour by French artist Jean
Despuljols in 1941 showing the
EFEO-restored west entrance to
Preah Khan

the most dislocated temple in the area [and one] can only progress by
climbing. The courtyards are filled with the remains of collapsed towers. The vaults fill the galleries they once covered [...] everywhere
sandstone covers the trees [i.e., the tree roots], the trees cause the collapse of the sandstone, within a greenish atmosphere striated by the
piercing shafts of sunlight, as if under water.

Thirty years of work resulted in the gradual disappearance of most of the
forest at Preah Khan, hand in hand with the progress of the restoration, and
with one of its corollaries: the protection of the temple from falling trees.
Although this was a twentieth-century preoccupation, this procedure has
become less and less acceptable, since it has relegated the forest to the periph-
ery of the temple while at the same time theatricalizing it. This strategy,
currently being implemented at Ta Prohm, Beng Mealea and Banteay Chhmar,

is related to the policy of promoting the image of a flagship temple during the Sihanouk period (1954–70). Several scenes from Richard Brooks's film *Lord Jim* (1965), starring Peter O'Toole, were filmed in Preah Kahn; this was the first Hollywood production in Angkor. Three years later, in 1968, some unforgettable sequences of *Ombres sur Angkor* ("Shadows over Angkor") were directed by King Norodom Sihanouk in the same temple.

Preah Khan's status as an Angkorian icon also stems from its historical value, unveiled throughout the progress of Angkorian research studies. At the same time that the clearing began, the French art historian Philippe Stern published his thesis in Paris, correctly identifying the position of the Bayon in the evolution of Khmer art. This completely undermined the previously established chronology of monuments by dating the creation of the Bayon two centuries later than had been believed, and Stern dated similarly all temples in the same style, including Preah Khan. This new chronology was verified a year later by Georges Coedès. Although Henri Marchal was at first unconvinced, he soon came to agree with Stern, noting, however:

> I conclude the following, which has been haunting me [...] these monuments which have been moved over centuries in one block, and to which a date has been firmly attached, do not form an ensemble built under the same reign. What is the date of the Louvre in Paris? Some say it is of the François I era, others [that it dates to] Napoleon III – and they are both right.

Although Marchal was wrong to compare Jayavarman VII to Napoleon III, he underlined a historical issue that then became a major one for all Bayon-style monuments: the complexity of their architectural modification. Cleaning and reconstruction work at Preah Khan showed that it was founded by Jayavarman VII, and this was confirmed by the foundation stele, discovered in November 1939 during clearance of the *gopura* of the first enclosure. Work there also disclosed numerous remains, showing that the original configuration had undergone a major transformation. The curators' logs are filled with references to reused blocks, structures added to structures and so on. As Marchal ironically proposed with a neologism, there were unaccountable traces of "*buddoclastes*", or obliterated Buddhist representations.

Over the years the architectural chronology begun by the French architect Henri Parmentier, the founder of Angkor Conservation, came to agree with Stern's studies of the stylistic development, resulting in a distinction between several periods within the Bayon style. Later research refined this approach, but some specialists propose that it is now time to look also into the history and chronology of these monuments, among which Preah Khan plays a major role. These studies will use new methodological tools and extend beyond the reign of Jayavarman VII to a largely unknown period of Angkorian history – the one that led to the abandonment of Angkor. In this area much additional clearing away of the undergrowth will undoubtedly be necessary.

# World Monuments Fund at Preah Khan

John H. Stubbs

Since 1989 World Monuments Fund (WMF) has worked to preserve and present the monumental remains of Preah Khan in a project that has influenced both the site and the changing dynamic of local and international conservation interests working at Angkor. From the beginning of WMF's regular fieldwork at Preah Khan in 1991 the organization's efforts have focused on developing appropriate methods for stabilizing, conserving and presenting the surviving elements of this large temple site in ways that would inform Angkorian heritage conservation in general. During this period a plethora of conservation interventions have been carried out, based on conservation priorities, visitor needs at the site and the realities of conducting such work in a country slowly rebuilding itself after a decade of social upheaval.

The first 10 years of the WMF Preah Khan Conservation Program proved successful beyond all expectations. After settling into a routine of annual fieldwork and related training activities, the organization became engaged in conserving three additional sites: the temples of Ta Som, Phnom Bakheng and a portion of Angkor Wat. Other significant projects involving WMF prior to the year 2000 included the initiation in 1994 of space and airborne radar imaging at Angkor, documentation and site preparation for featuring the island temple Neak Pean located in the Jayatataka (the northern *baray*), the launch of the Center for Khmer Studies in the provincial seat of Siem Reap and the development of a preliminary conservation master plan for the outlying temple of Banteay Chhmar.

Conservation work conducted at Preah Khan during the period 2000–09 addressed in earnest the added task of interpreting the site for vastly increasing numbers of both national and international visitors. This latter effort culminated in the opening of a refurbished Visitors' Center in November 2008.

Seen from the beginning as a showcase project, the WMF Preah Khan Conservation Program entailed a number of attendant activities related to training and international advocacy. Working alongside dozens of young

Khmer architects, archaeologists, engineers and other trainees was a constant stream of heritage conservation professionals from different countries, who participated in as many as four key field missions a year, addressing issues ranging from general supervision (project planning, international liaison work with authorities and ensuring high work standards) to problem-solving at a technical level (engineering solutions, bio-deterioration studies, computerized documentation). Considerable time was devoted to working with other international heritage conservation teams and with staff and officials at APSARA (the Authority for the Protection and Management of Angkor and the Region of Siem Reap), who since 1994 have been in charge of all conservation and tourism activities within the greater Angkor area. Through these formative years in the professional management of Cambodia's premier cultural heritage attraction many techniques have been developed for enhanced field operations and the exchange of information, with the aim of furthering "best practice" in conserving and presenting ancient Khmer architectural remains and their sites.

WMF's activities at Angkor in general, and at Preah Khan in particular, can be described as comprising a long-range field programme, comparable to complex archaeological or architectural conservation programmes elsewhere in the world. The organization's first 15 years of work at Angkor evolved from project-scoping and mobilization missions, led by consulting

British architect and field project manager, John Sanday, and the Vice-President of WMF's Field Projects, John H. Stubbs, to the present team of young professionals, led by the materials conservation expert, Konstanze von zur Mühlen, who serves as the WMF Field Projects Manager in Cambodia, and Glenn Boornazian, consulting Director of Technical Conservation in Cambodia, based in New York. Numerous Cambodian project managers and staff have served vital roles over the years, one of whom, Cheam Phally, has actively participated in WMF's conservation work at Angkor since 1992.

One distinction of WMF's long involvement in Cambodia is that it was the first Western heritage conservation organization to work at Angkor since the country's devastating civil war from 1975 to 1979 and its aftermath. (The Archaeological Survey of India conducted restoration work at Angkor Wat from 1988 to 1993.) On the signing of the Paris Peace Accords in 1991, and the start of the United Nations' largest and most expensive peacekeeping operation to date, the United Nations Educational and Scientific Organization (UNESCO) began to play a major role in Cambodia. Among its many assistance programmes were several to aid in cultural heritage protection. Among its first achievements was its vital role in establishing APSARA, which was set up by royal decree in 1994. This politically independent quasi-governmental authority, which oversees every aspect of Angkor as well as a few adjacent sites, was created as a condition of the greater Angkor archaeological area being placed on the UNESCO World Heritage list in 1993.

From the beginning of APSARA's presence as a heritage protection convener and administrative body, WMF's experiences were shared in support of APSARA's goals of harmonizing conservation methodologies throughout Angkor. Annual proposals by WMF to conduct discrete conservation interventions were revised to reflect APSARA's evolving systems of communication, documentation and review. Remarkably little changed in the way WMF conducted its field projects, except for some changes to advocacy and site interpretation efforts that needed to be harmonized with new plans for presenting Angkor in its totality. Site maintenance, security and ticketing operations radically improved from the mid-1990s, in response to Angkor's increasing popularity as a cultural heritage tourism destination in Asia.

Today APSARA is a robust heritage site management body and is considered a model of its type. The APSARA authority, and initiatives such as those by WMF, along with several other international heritage protection efforts at Angkor, have helped foster a new generation of Khmer heritage conservation experts with skills in research, documentation, architectural and environmental conservation and tourism management.

OPPOSITE WMF's field team disengaging stones from the north-west courtyard of the west Vishnu complex, 1993

ABOVE Hoisting a fallen *borne* at the west processional entrance way, 1993

## Conservation by WMF at Preah Khan

During WMF's first mission to Angkor in December 1989 it was decided that Preah Khan could be an ideal starting point for WMF work in Cambodia and the region. With Ministry of Culture approval the second mission to Angkor

in 1991 marked the launch of a field project, in the belief that starting a programme of conservation work would prove exemplary. An approach was developed that took into account the fact that neither the then Ministry of Culture unit in charge of Angkor (which pre-dated APSARA) nor WMF had experience of conducting large archaeological site conservation work of this type. A methodology was devised that necessarily assumed minimal government support and allowed for the country's non-existent telecommunications and seriously compromised infrastructure, the difficulties of finding materials and trained personnel, and Cambodia's still extremely tenuous political condition. Detachments of the Cambodian national military continued to wrestle with Khmer Rouge stragglers in the Siem Reap region (which includes Angkor) until the end of 1993.

Owing to the devastating effects of the Khmer Rouge on the Cambodian population, any new initiative, including the recommencement of work at an ancient Khmer temple, meant assembling and training an entirely new local workforce for a wholly new system of protocols and requirements. These conditions shaped the management of the Preah Khan conservation effort in its first three years. Increasingly from 1994 WMF's task was to fit within

APSARA's new system of governance over Angkor. In this context the first decade of conservation work at Preah Khan served as a prototype for other initiatives, including showing by example what conserving a large ancient Khmer temple entails, and importantly, what is involved in developing sustainable heritage conservation projects at Angkor, where training is a key component.

Conservation master-planning began during Preah Khan Campaign I, in 1991, through the work of the Australian heritage conservation consultancy firm, Anglin & Cunliffe, who determined the initial physical and conceptual parameters for conservation treatment of the site. This work was expanded on by WMF staff in 1992 to reflect WMF's strategy for financing the project primarily from the private sector. By the start of Field Campaign III in 1993, the mapping of priority conservation projects, testing at several trial interventions, development of a cadre of site workers and regular international consultants, and a 10-year master plan for stabilizing the architectural remains at the site were in hand. The project evolved from a project identification phase to a planning and testing phase, to general mobilization and implementation of a complex and sizeable conservation programme. During this period crucially important archival and historical research was carried out, documentation of conditions "as found" was conducted, pilot projects were initiated, methods of documentation were perfected and the clearance of 15 years of accumulated jungle overgrowth was achieved. Over the same period a relationship developed between the WMF team working in Cambodia and deans of archaeology and architecture at the Royal University of Fine Arts (RUFA) in Phnom Penh, as a result of which an agreement was reached that Preah Khan would be used for extra-mural teaching of students interested in architectural heritage protection. A plan of action was developed, and commitments were made by both sponsors and owners to move forward in a series of annual campaigns that continue to the present time.

*Defining an approach*

The conservation philosophy of WMF at Angkor derives from the challenges recognized at the vast archaeological park at the start of the organization's work there. WMF's aim at Angkor has been to demonstrate methods of preserving and presenting this cultural heritage site of world importance that respect both local interests and appropriate international conservation principles and procedures. Owing to the circumstances, help in the training of a new generation of conservators would be a hallmark of the approach.

Given the conservation challenges posed by the abandoned stone ruins of the large site as found in 1989, WMF's approach was to continue the conservation efforts of the École Française d'Extrême-Orient (EFEO), with a number of modified techniques, aimed at stabilizing and featuring the key parts of the site as a partial ruin. An emphasis was placed on the development of archaeological site maintenance techniques with a focus on training that would inform the conservation of other Khmer architectural heritage sites at Angkor and beyond. All conservation planning and interventions began with the documentation of the historic architectural fabric in its condition "as

OPPOSITE Temporary structural shoring within the principal east entrance *gopura*, 1993

LEFT A partially collapsed side corridor, south-west quadrant of Preah Khan

found". Selected building components and conditions merited the more extensive intervention of "partial restoration".

Additionally, WMF's comprehensive approach to conservation at Angkor has included presenting architectural ruins in the natural setting in which they are found, determining the aspects of greatest value and the significance of the site as a cultural resource for the benefit of local users and visitors, promulgating stone structure stabilization and restoration techniques for the benefit of local craftsmen and workers, and advocating for the deterrence of theft from, and vandalism of, Cambodia's architectural heritage. Site safety has always been a concern: for instance, conditions along main passageways deemed dangerous to visitors were cordoned off with warning signs until they could be attended to, on a priority basis.

WMF seeks to pass Preah Khan on to future generations in a state similar to that in which it was found in its preserved natural setting, having used discreet and modern methods of conservation that will extend the life of the monument. The Preah Khan Conservation programme strives to conserve one of Angkor's key temples while aiding the local population by providing jobs, technical assistance and cultural exchange.

TOP Khmer architect
Cheam Phally verifying field
measurements, 1993

ABOVE International consultants
from Integrated Conservation
Resources, Inc. teaching the
Khmer project team digital
survey techniques for mapping
stone conditions, 2004

## Training

From WMF's first mission to Angkor in December 1989 it was clear that training a new generation of professionals and craftspeople was essential. In response, all approaches to conservation at Preah Khan, and all of WMF's other subsequent activities at Angkor, assumed that training would be a major component of the organization's efforts in the field. During the first years of fieldwork WMF's project managers strived to create partnerships with what remained of the country's decimated institutions of higher learning. The only educational facility physically to survive the Khmer Rouge years where there was any hope of quick reactivation was the Royal University of Fine Arts (RUFA), an adjunct of the National Museum in Phnom Penh. WMF staff witnessed at first hand the early days of this institution's revival, when facilities were meagre. There was no electricity, no teaching equipment and only three known surviving teachers or graduates from the pre-war years. With volunteer help and increasing aid from UNESCO and other organizations, by the mid-1990s a semblance of the RUFA's college education system was back in place, just in time for a flood of new students and with more on the way.

It was in this context that WMF worked with teachers of architecture and archaeology at the RUFA from 1991 to supplement the classroom education of students in both these disciplines with field experience at Angkor's Preah Khan. Based on interviews and staff recommendations, an initial group of six graduate students was selected and allowed to work at Angkor under WMF's sponsorship and care. In Siem Reap these student interns were accommodated at WMF House and paid a modest stipend, in return for assisting the international team in documenting selected areas of Preah Khan before, during and after architectural stabilization work with measured drawings and photographs. Additional responsibilities included helping the international team in supervising and communicating with local Khmer work crews and assistance with all manner of logistical matters. At the same time a system of mentoring was developed whereby foreign team members assisted the Khmer interns with aspects of their education and career interests.

Through this experience a rich process of exchange between Khmer and foreign teachers developed further, with WMF staff and consultants giving lectures to entire classes at the RUFA. Further assistance was offered in the form of advice on writing theses and specialty workshops conducted at WMF House, where certificates of attendance were given. The same venue was used for conducting several *charrettes* (intensive project planning meetings that engage respondents), at which Khmer student interns and young professionals played an important part. One of the more fruitful *charrettes* was conducted in 1998, which determined the feasibility and eventual creation of the Center for Khmer Studies, Cambodia's first postgraduate research and training facility in the arts and humanities. Other significant international meetings conducted by WMF at Angkor included a Planning Workshop on Values-Based Conservation and Interpretation at Preah Khan, in 2000, and a Scholars' Conference on the History and Significance of Phnom Bakheng, in 2002.

Other formats for supplementary training were also developed, especially for more advanced Khmer professional colleagues. Several graduating Khmer

LEFT Removing undergrowth
and soil accumulation at the
west wall of Preah Khan, 1992

TOP The Two-Storey Pavilion
before vegetation removal, 1992

ABOVE The Two-Storey Pavilion
after vegetation removal, 1994

architects and archaeologists were supported in their participation in architectural heritage training programmes abroad at the University of Hawaii, the
Institute of Earthquake and Engineering Seismology at the St. Cyril and
Methodius University in Skopje, Macedonia, and at Taliesin West in Arizona.
In 1997–98 the first dean of the school of architecture at the RUFA, Hor Lat,
was sponsored by a member of WMF's International Council to complete his
formal architectural training at the Polytechnic University of Turin.

Equally important was WMF's commitment to train numbers of workers
and craftspeople of all ages in architectural conservation on site at Preah
Khan. Since 1991 over 250 local craftsmen and labourers have worked for
WMF, first at Preah Khan and later at the organization's other projects at Ta
Som, Angkor Wat and Phnom Bakheng. Their involvement in these projects
has ranged from site clearance and maintenance work to every aspect of structural stabilization and conservation measures.

The on-site training of craftsmen at Preah Khan was conducted with
respect for traditional working methods. WMF technical staff, assisted by
Khmer architecture or engineering interns, determined and designed specific

projects for teams of fieldworkers, who worked in cadres of between eight and 12 men under the direction of *chefs de chantier* (team leaders, usually senior craftsmen in stone construction). During the early years at Preah Khan, when fieldwork entailed the removal of vegetation and general site preparation, as many as 125 people worked at the site. With this system of organization scores of important conservation projects and sub-projects were accomplished. Interventions ranged in size, from the temporary propping-up of structures threatening to collapse, to clearing away fallen stones and debris, to complex *in situ* repairs of large architectural components and entire structures.

## Conservation interventions, 1992–2008

### Site-wide structural propping
Based on the results of a site-wide survey by senior project engineer, Predrag Gavrilovic, working in concert with the Project Director and architect, John Sanday, structural risk assessments were made of the entire Preah Khan complex. A prioritized ranking of building conservation challenges that assessed plans for opening further parts of the site to the public gave shape to a series of annual conservation campaigns.

In several instances the threat of structural collapse could not wait until the completion of the conservation planning process. Structural support using treated timber to shore up buildings at risk began during the first WMF field mission in 1991, with a system that has been used continuously since then. Timber props held tight with pairs of folding wooden wedges were often all that was needed to hold a structural component in place until it could

*Evolution of a structural repair*

BELOW The south porch of Preah Khan's principal east *gopura* as found in October 1992

BELOW RIGHT Emergency propping of the south porch of Preah Khan's east *gopura*, November 1992

be properly attended to. The roving structural propping team at Preah Khan certainly prevented collapse and further damage to a number of structures at the site.

In other instances more sophisticated designs for timber propping were required, for example where lengths of wall or corbelled vaulting threatened to give way. In a few cases steel pipework shoring intended to last for a period of several years was installed, as in the case of the central towers of the east and west *gopuras* at Preah Khan's fourth enclosure wall. The propping methods developed at Preah Khan not only provide added protection for the site's increasing numbers of visitors but also reflect practicality; "a stitch in time saves nine" is an important principle in this kind of stone repair work, since preserving the authenticity of building materials in their original positions is always preferred.

*East gopura, south portico, third enclosure wall*
The south portico of Preah Khan's principal east *gopura* – the main architectural elevation of the entire complex – was on the verge of collapse from tree damage and was chosen as a pilot project for extensive structural repairs in 1993. The programme entailed bracing the post-and-beam structure within a rigid frame of steel scaffolding, designed so that the structure's massive lintel and gable stones could be lifted above their normal positions and lowered again on their original porch columns after they were righted. Such an innovative method, as opposed to taking the whole assembly down to ground-level and re-erecting it, saved significant time and labour costs. This relatively small pilot project proved to be the first of many *in situ* structural repairs for the architectural fabric of Preah Khan.

*The conservation process*

BELOW LEFT Righting the tilting columns after the lintels of the porch are lifted *in situ*, October 1993

BELOW Completed stabilization of the south porch of Preah Khan's entrance *gopura*, January 1994

Collapsed roof stones along Preah Khan's north axial passageway, 1996

A similar, though more extensive, shrine porch and fronton (decorative pediment above a portal) repair project was conducted on the west side of the north porch of the east *gopura* at Preah Khan's fourth enclosure wall, near which everyone accessing the site from the principal east entrance must pass. A similar intervention entailing partial disassembly and re-erection of a fronton, its supporting lintel and the conservation of two stone *dvarapalas* (guardian figures) was conducted at the west entry to the temple complex.

*Wall repairs*
Along the hundreds of metres of laterite and sandstone walls that form the four separate enclosures at Preah Khan were, and still are, a number of sections that have collapsed under the weight of falling trees. In areas where practical and aesthetic considerations merited restoration, several breaks in the walls were repaired by repositioning fallen stone blocks using newly cut laterite blocks as required. Rebuilding damaged walls to their original height of 3.5 metres proved to be a relatively simple matter where wall foundations remained intact. The experience of repairing walls and a number of other damaged structures has heightened WMF's appreciation of the importance of tree management at Preah Khan. Such work has entailed the monitoring, pruning and occasional removal of unhealthy large trees threatening damage to structures.

## Clearance of passageways

Over the course of the first decade of fieldwork at Preah Khan a number of passageways were cleared in order to provide safer and improved circulation through the site. The principal east-west axial way required relatively little work; however, the north section of main north-south axial way also leading to Preah Khan's *sanctum sanctorum* required extensive intervention. The opening-up of corridors and connecting passageways blocked by partially collapsed walls and corbelled roof stones is delicate work and can be quite dangerous. The Khmer fieldworkers proved to be masters at lifting and sorting heaps of collapsed stone and restoring them to their original positions. With Preah Khan today being among the most popular sites for visitors to Angkor, the early decision to improve site circulation by opening all the site's principal passageways has proved to be one of WMF's wisest decisions.

## The Hall of Dancers

One the most impressive buildings at Preah Khan is the so-called Hall of Dancers, named in modern times after its finely carved lintels, which depict dancing figures. It is the first grand space encountered on entering the temple from the east. Cruciform in plan, the central area of this building was once covered by a cross-vault that measured some 4.2 x 3.8 metres, making it one of the largest of all known Khmer corbelled-vault enclosures. Its tall, broad spans were supported by an ingenious use of supporting galleries at a lower level, which form four small open cloisters at its corners, and a system of stone struts that held corbelled roof vaults in place in a manner not dissimilar (at least visually) to how flying buttresses support the upper reaches of some European Gothic cathedrals. In each of the four resultant columned cloister areas are the remains of shallow open-air basins that were connected

BELOW LEFT Structural repairs to the east corridor of the Hall of Dancers, 1995

BELOW Stabilization of partially reconstructed roof stones of the Hall of Dancers, 1995

ABOVE The Wat Bo Dance Troupe performing in Preah Khan's Hall of Dancers, 1996

OPPOSITE The stabilized inner portal of the west entrance of the Hall of Dancers, 1996

to the site's surface water drainage system. (One may speculate whether these basins contained water, at least at certain times of the year, which would have further enriched the aesthetic appeal of this majestic structure.) When operational, these small columned cloisters would have served as natural light sources at the corners of the Hall of Dancers and may have provided added ventilation and acoustic qualities.

Given the prominence of this structure, necessary structural stabilization work was conducted at several locations here between 1995 and 1998 that provided a good example of WMF's conservation philosophy of stabilizing Preah Khan as a partial ruin. Interventions included the partial disassembly of the south colonnade at the east end of the structure, and repairs to cracked lintels and split columns elsewhere. Enough of each part of the Hall of Dancers remains to allow its visitors easily to imagine the magnificence of this important space. Throughout 2003 WMF was permitted to stage modest Khmer dance performances in the Hall of Dancers. The experience of viewing modern costumed dancers performing to traditional gamelan music among stone carvings of the same subject was nothing short of magical for those in attendance.

### Miscellaneous structural repair techniques and projects

The stone structures that comprise the ruins of Preah Khan were formed using a range of wall, column and vaulting techniques that are often more complex than they appear at first sight. At the time of Preah Khan's construction the Khmer tradition of trabeated (post-and-beam) architecture supporting corbelled vaulting had been practised for nearly three centuries at Angkor. Buildings such as Preah Khan, dating from the era of Jayavarman VII, are often characterized as being a type of construction that was erected more quickly, with less attention to detail and more short cuts in materials, than structures from earlier eras, such as Banteay Srei, Beng Mealea and Angkor Wat.

In seeking to address necessary structural repairs at Preah Khan in an efficient, low-tech and cost-effective way, project engineers and squads of Khmer workers developed systems for pinning cracked or broken stones using non-ferrous metal dowels and other inserts. This technique usually entails cleaning fractured surfaces, drilling holes in both sides that facilitate perfect alignment, inserting either fibreglass or stainless-steel dowels embedded in epoxide adhesives and concealing all work as necessary with identical stone inserts or composite patching. This method proved to be standard practice from 1994 on. Similarly detailed through-bolting of square splitting columns was also perfected at about the same time. Similar techniques were used on smaller-scale architectural sculpture, such as broken *naga* railing details and the pairs of free-standing *dvarapala* figures at Preah Khan's west and south entrance *gopuras*. In a select few repairs new stone was used in stabilization work at Preah Khan, and then only when it played an important aesthetic or structural role.

Shifted corbelled vault roof stones have been reset and fallen ones re-erected in several areas of Preah Khan, often in relation to opening and securing corridor structures. Occasionally this delicate vault stone stabiliza-

tion work was done *in situ*, high off the ground, using structural scaffolding as an elevated work platform. The teams of Khmer carpenters in performing this work developed a real proficiency at this often dangerous task.

The first conservation intervention involving an arrangement of structures was undertaken at the Vishnu complex, located in the west part of Preah Khan. Cleaning and stabilization work was done at several different locations in this part of the temple with a view to making the west entrance to the temple safer, more physically accessible and more intelligable as an architectural ensemble. Particular projects entailed stabilizing and repairing fallen or damaged ornamental frontons, repairing failed building components that restored structural integrity to unstable adjacent areas, and disassembling and reassembling the stone roofing system of a wide connecting corridor. More of a fine art repair and conservation operation was undertaken in the "re-restoration" of a *dvarapala* statue prominently located at the portal of Preah Khan's west Vishnu complex.

*The dharmasala*

Located approximately 75 metres north-east of the stone paved entrance to Preah Khan's principal east *gopura* and facing the site's east access way is a

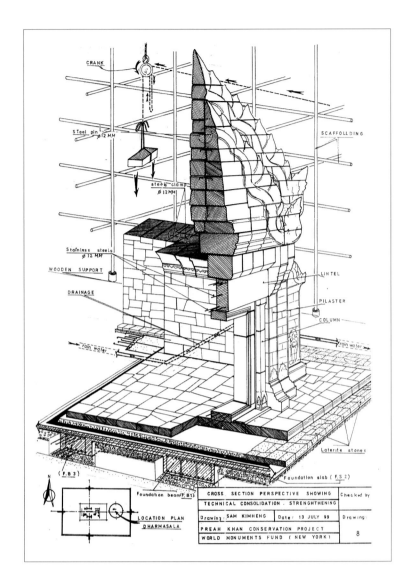

special building type called a *dharmasala*, which probably served to house the *agni*, or Holy Flame. Other speculations on the use of such *dharmasalas* during Angkorian times include their having been pilgrims' rest houses or places for receiving food offerings at the temple.

In 1996 the Preah Khan *dharmasala* was discovered to be on the verge of collapse, owing to outward slippage of the structure's northern wall footing and separation of its entire east wall. Propping and remedial foundation repair work temporarily arrested these problems while funds were raised to address the building as a whole. The east wall that forms the primary entrance to this pavilion was documented, disassembled and re-erected on a new, buried reinforced-concrete footing. Less extensive stabilization measures were used at the structure's west wall. Hardly any of these interventions, which were undertaken between 1998 and 2002, are visible today, owing to their detailing. Aiding their invisibility is subsequent surface micro-biological growth, which is considered harmless. Today the *dharmasala* of Preah Khan represents one of the few almost completely intact ancient Khmer structures to be found at Angkor.

OPPOSITE Design for repair of the *dharmasala*, 1999

LEFT Purposefully utilized "low-technology" in the recording of Preah Khan's *dharmasala*, 1996. Base drawings of the building's elevations were developed from tracing scaled straight-on photographs.

BELOW The *dharamasala*, with temporary shoring, 1997

*Garuda* (restored in 2008) at the south-west corner of Preah Khan

## Conservation of garudas

Among the most notable features of all the rich architectural and sculptural remains at Preah Khan are the site's 72 magnificent stone *garuda* ("guardian birdman") figures that adorn the temple's outermost protective wall. These mythical beaked and feathered man-bird images, each one holding a pair of multi-headed *nagas* (serpents) in its talons, are spaced at 35-metre intervals along Preah Khan's 3 kilometres long, 3.5 metres high, laterite wall over-looking the temple's perimeter moat. As a metaphor for the relationship between the celestial and earthly realms, Preah Khan's display of monumental stone *garudas* added protective powers and distinction to the monastic complex within.

The *garudas* of Preah Khan are nearly identical in appearance, except for the four located at the enclosure wall corners, whose wings are folded back at right angles. After nearly 500 years of abandonment many of these finely carved sandstone figures are detached from their laterite wall backing as a result of termite infestations in the joints of these dissimilar materials. A number of *garudas* and their associated wall-lengths were discovered to have been damaged by falling trees.

From 1998, in a programme begun by project manager, John Sanday, World Monuments Fund launched an "Adopt a *Garuda*" programme as a fundraising scheme for the Preah Khan Conservation project in general. In the first 12 years of the programme some 28 *garuda* conservation projects have been sponsored by individuals or groups of donors. The *garuda* conservation programme has been handled in essentially two multi-year campaigns of work. The first entailed the clearance of both sides of Preah Khan's perimeter wall from jungle encroachment to determine general conservation priorities, after which nearly 18 of these sculptures were addressed. From 2005 stone conservation specialist, Konstanze von zur Mühlen, assisting the Garuda Conservation Program project manager, architect Cheam Phally, developed new and improved techniques for conserving the *garudas* of Preah Khan. The Preah Khan Visitors' Center holds a special display on the current Garuda Conservation Program, complete with a list of donors who have supported this important work.

## Archaeology at Preah Khan

Owing to the ample number of conservation priorities that are evident just walking through Preah Khan, most archaeology done over the past two decades has been of the "above grade" type and not the usual subterranean or "below grade" type. Most excavation during WMF's tenure has been devoted to disengaging partially buried buildings – especially fallen stonework – from jungle overgrowth and soil overburden (humus derived from leaf debris), which in some areas had accumulated over a period of nearly five centuries. Such work, termed *dégagement* by WMF's French predecessors, is more a matter of debris removal than of orthodox archaeology.

Archaeological soundings and larger excavations were performed in selected areas by the project team archaeologist, Chan Chamroeun, mainly in support of efforts to conserve Preah Khan's monumental remains. Typical examples of archaeological work done by WMF include investigation of the depths and designs of building foundations at the site's central tower and exposure of the remains of the large, paved west jetty area of the Jayatataka, which once served as a boat landing. The archaeological strata of each of these sites revealed construction details and occasional other finds, including pottery shards. Soundings in other locations revealed pottery shards, stone architectural details, bronze construction fittings and baked clay roof tiles.

As revealing as the discovery and excavation work at the west jetty (1996–97) were Chamroeun's surface surveys of Preah Khan's former residential precincts that surrounded the temple proper between the first and second enclosure walls. Street and housing patterns were partially discerned by the mapping of surface anomalies, especially indentations revealing former water collection tanks (pools) that served individual houses and possibly larger structures. One discovery made during the general site survey work in the north-west quadrant of the site was the foundation remains of the east-facing Preah Khan Wat *vihara* (a larger Buddhist temple, the place of worship for its Buddhist monks), complete with its *sima* (boundary markers), which face in eight directions.

The largest and most important archaeological discovery made in April 1999 in the overgrown areas of Preah Khan was in the north-east quadrant, where a water basin was found that measured 26 x 51 metres, approximately 4 metres deep, lined with laterite stone steps. Large post holes and other evidence led Chamroeun to surmise that this could be another *vihara*, or possibly even part of a temporary royal palace at Preah Khan that served Jayavarman VII.

From the beginning of WMF's work at Preah Khan the assistance of archaeologists has been crucial, since carefully measured graphic documentation of "as found" appearances of buildings is always the first step in conservation programmes. Very detailed records of the condition of buildings both before and after stabilization and partial rebuilding work are constantly maintained in such projects. Since the beginning of the project thousands of drawings and photographs have been produced, which are indexed and on file at the WMF Preah Khan Archive in Siem Reap. Additionally, it was always the archaeologists, working in co-operation with Khmer work teams, who were best at understanding patterns of collapse and responding to questions about which stones came from where.

## Site management, presentation and interpretation

### Improvements to site circulation
A major goal from the commencement of WMF's fieldwork at Preah Khan was to prepare the site for improved site circulation and make it safer and more comprehendible for visitors. While most of the principal east-west axis through the site was found to be unobstructed at the time of WMF's start of work at Preah Khan, neither the north nor the south axial passageways was passable because of collapsed roof stones. During the first eight years of the

project considerable effort was devoted to the opening of these passageways. By 1999 access to the Central Shrine of Preah Khan from all four cardinal directions was possible again for the first time in hundreds of years. The opening of the entire site's key passageways has played an important role in preventing problems of congestion among the site's increasing numbers of visitors. Importantly, one may now enter Preah Khan via one *gopura* and exit from another, thus avoiding cross-circulation and backtracking.

### Nature observed and conserved

The magnificent forest setting of Preah Khan is one of the site's main assets. For all that is said about the large trees and jungle setting of Preah Khan's sister temple, Ta Prohm, it is fair to say that Preah Khan today offers a comparable blend of architecture and nature, especially in its southern half. Tree foliage overhead and walls of forest beyond the temple provide a picturesque context for the monumental remains of the large site and also provide a cooler and more constant micro-climate which benefits the temple's architectural remains.

During Field Campaign III, in 1994, the Khmer-American forester, Ronnie Yimsut, conducted a comprehensive survey of trees and plants within the first enclosure wall at Preah Khan and even developed a large tree health inspection programme. The following year Yimsut directed the cutting of nature trails through the site and was the first at Angkor to place wayside markers identifying plant materials using their Latin taxonomical, Khmer and English names. Over 40 species of tree and plant materials were identified, ranging from the tall and highly prized *dipterocarpus* and giant ficus trees (*tetrameles nudiflora*), which rise to over 30 metres in height, to bamboos and medicinal plants.

### Site signage and the Preah Khan Visitors' Center

From the early 1990s the WMF project team has observed increasing numbers of visitors to Preah Khan, drawn to the temple's remarkable display of sculptural details and impressive views through long corridors and passageways in its rich jungle setting. Bilingual wayside markers have proved useful both in highlighting key points of interest and safety hazards throughout the site and in describing ongoing conservation work in particular areas. In 1994 project manager, John Sanday, set up a modest visitors' centre in a timber building with a thatched roof along the site's west entrance path. In it were displayed maps, images of work in progress and WMF's project publications. This structure proved to be the first of several structures built or renovated in this location.

In November 2008 the present Preah Khan Visitors' Center was completed, in a renovated building, with improved exhibits and text panels in Khmer and English. It is a deliberately "green" design, and its interiors use natural lighting. Themes on display include physical and historical descriptions of Preah Khan, explanations of conservation and documentation techniques, and presentations on special topics such as the Garuda Conservation Program and the significance of Preah Khan for Cambodians today.

OPPOSITE The north axial corridor after clearance, 1999

RIGHT A prized *dipterocarpus* tree at Preah Khan

BELOW A pair of giant ficus trees (*tetrameles nudiflora*) straddling the south corridor of Preah Khan's east entrance *gopura*, 2003

The reception desk at the centre also offers Angkor-related guidebooks and reference books, and a simple brochure about the site and its main features. The supporters of WMF's conservation and training work at Preah Khan and other projects at Angkor are credited in this location.

*Site maintenance and security*
Maintenance of the very large site of Preah Khan in its somewhat remote location at the northern edge of the Angkor Archaeological Park has been a constant concern. When the site was reopened with improved access in the early 1990s, a correct balance and frequency of maintenance operations had to be determined. In the early years WMF was exclusively responsible for site maintenance at Preah Khan. It was established that a well maintained and tidy site was of paramount importance, out of respect for this spiritual place in its remarkable jungle setting. Today the upkeep of the site is a more complicated affair, in large part because of the increasing numbers of visitors.

In trying to develop effective site presentation measures even the most mundane matters were considered, such as salary levels and work schedules for maintenance personnel and locations of waste receptacles. Hiring mostly local villagers as maintenance personnel proved especially successful, since it also engendered pride and interest among locals in helping to protect the site.

Detachments of military personnel at the site for security purposes in the early years have given way to trained APSARA personnel, who control entrances and keep an eye on tourists, who are free to meander almost at will among the temple's extensive remains. A spate of thefts of architectural sculpture at Preah Khan and other temples in the early 1990s was halted with the introduction of added site security and the establishment of a mobile and armed heritage police force, which patrols Angkor at all hours.

## Documentation

*Graphic documentation*
A key objective of the first WMF field mission to Preah Khan was to verify and update the graphic and photographic documentation of the site produced earlier by French scholars as a means of expanding on their work to preserve and present the site. The bulk of archival information developed over the years by scholars of the EFEO was not available to the WMF team until 1995; however, a published general site plan served from the time of the first mission as a basis for defining the physical parameters of the overall project and charting conditions at the site. An archive of drawings and photographs produced by WMF from the beginning of its involvement was created, which at present contains some 8,000 items. In the belief that using traditional graphic documentation techniques would be the best means of training Khmer interns, hand measurements of buildings and the transcription of this information on to scale drawings have been the predominant methods of architectural documentation. Plans, sections and elevations were prepared for over 200

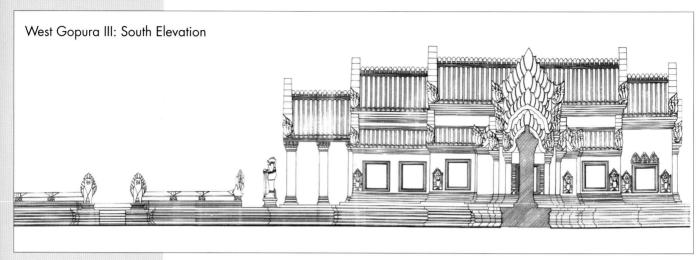

West Gopura III: South Elevation

West Gopura III: West Elevation

Drawings by the Khmer field team of the south and west elevations of Preah Khan's west principal entrance *gopura*

conservation interventions conducted at the site. Since 2002 most new field drawings have been immediately transcribed on to a Computer Assisted Drawing (CAD) system, which has greatly facilitated information storage and referencing, overlays, improved graphic presentations and easier quantity and quality surveys. Annual reports, presentations of proposed conservation work and occasional published articles represent other forms of project documentation.

### Reporting

In the period from 1992 to 1999 standardized Field Reports for the Preah Khan Conservation Project, plus separate appendices, were produced, in which every accomplishment was recorded and filed on an annual basis. From the year 2000 the documentation of conservation actions at Preah Khan, especially completion reports, has been recorded via illustrated presentations to APSARA at its annual meetings of the International Coordinating Council. In 2004 a boxed set of WMF's project documentation on Preah Khan, consisting of all annual reports, appendices and related material, was presented to the APSARA archive. The majority of these documents are available for viewing as PDF files on WMF's website.

## Specialist analyses

Various specialist analyses, research projects, workshops and demonstration projects have characterized WMF's work at Angkor, in the belief that sound research and the sharing of the resulting knowledge were among the main aims of the organization's mission in Cambodia. Such research methodologies lend themselves well to a large, complicated and important cultural heritage site as Preah Khan and, by extension, can often be applied to Angkor as a whole. Most international field missions entailed specific tasks, involving problem-solving, such as a bio-deterioration analysis conducted by Frank Preusser (1995), specialist analyses of stone conservation issues by stone conservator, Paolo Pagnin (1998), analyses of landscape features and possibilities for nature trails conducted by Ronnie Yimsut (1994–95), flora and fauna graphic documentation by Andrew Dennis (1997–2000), whole site illustration and spatial analyses by architect, Kevin Sarring (1997) and the organization of space-borne ground-penetrating radar analyses at Angkor instigated by John Stubbs (1994). Engineer, Predrag Gavrilovic, produced a compendium of structural repair techniques in 1996, which were later presented at three international conferences. A workshop that resulted in a new 10-year conservation management plan for Preah Khan was conducted by Sharon Sullivan in 2000, which emphasized the need for site conservation and interpretation based on heritage values. In 2007 a revised programme for the conservation of the rare collection of *garuda* figures was produced by conservator, Konstanze von zur Mühlen, and architect, Cheam Phally.

## Advocacy

Being an international organization devoted to the conservation of the world's significant architectural heritage, World Monuments Fund has consistently advocated for architectural conservation and related assistance to the Kingdom of Cambodia's request for help in 1989. In the early years especially, during Cambodia's very tenuous social stability, when a return to peaceful conditions was by no means certain, efforts by WMF to help there developed to become a focal interest of the organization. Participation at nearly all international conferences on Angkor was viewed as essential by WMF in the spirit of wishing to co-operate with other international teams aiding Cambodia's efforts to regain its footing as a civil society. Through WMF's position as a non-governmental organization (NGO), with projects in many other countries, and as a voice for the field, a number of presentations were made at venues with the aim of gaining new supporters of heritage protection in Cambodia. Lectures, publications and exhibitions offered to a range of audiences have been regular activities of WMF for nearly two decades. The organization has seen attitudes about Cambodia change from its being viewed, in the early 1990s, as a place where one feared for one's safety to the country being a "hot destination" for *au courant* travellers in the mid-1990s and now being a "must-see" tourist destination.

From 1994 WMF conducted tours of Angkor for its constituency sometimes as frequently as three times per year. Countless guided tours of Preah Khan and other parts of Angkor have been provided by the Cambodia-based staff of WMF over the years as a means of promoting Angkor and sharing WMF's experiences. WMF's policy all along has been to train and advocate for effective heritage conservation, and to share these experiences as widely as possible.

## Preah Khan into the future

Given Preah Khan's position among the key historic Angkorian sites, and the level of national and international heritage protection that is afforded today to the World Heritage Site of Angkor, it is safe to assume that Preah Khan's future as a revered architectural heritage site is secure. As such, any plans for the future of the site should view its treatment mainly a matter of maintaining the status quo. While there remains plenty to do in terms of further stabilization, interpretation and monitoring protection of the site in general, the key interventions that lie ahead should be reserved to discreet conservation and maintenance measures.

A key aim in architectural conservation projects is to preserve the integrity and character of such special places from the vicissitudes of human and

BELOW Exterior of the rebuilt Preah Khan Visitors' Center, 2010

OPPOSITE Interpretive displays at the Preah Khan Visitors' Center

natural threats. In this instance the two areas of focus that should be addressed most urgently from this point forward involve preventative conservation measures, in particular guarding against "tourist wear" and additional structural failures, and working to better feature the site of Preah Khan in its entirety. Both of these objectives will demand the regular on-site presence of experienced and capable teams charged with the task, in the manner of site maintenance teams who manage large archaeological ruins elsewhere in the world, be it the Forum in Rome or Tikal, Guatemala.

Visitors' surveys and comments received over the years have revealed that Preah Khan is among the favourite destinations of visitors to Angkor. Given the special qualities of its several unique artistic features, its size and design, its jungle setting and the fact that Preah Khan is situated on the north edge of Angkor's *grand circuit*, the site will probably retain its character as one of the most peaceful and beautiful settings of all the Angkorian sites. Preserving this overall quality is of paramount importance.

Fortunately Preah Khan plays an active role in the lives of Cambodian nationals today, since it is considered a sacred site by many who visit it. The religious associations of Preah Khan endow the site with even greater value as a special destination, which should further ensure its preservation. In this

connection the recent WMF interventions to improve access, provide safer conditions for visitors and offer basic interpretation via the Preah Khan Visitors' Center and wayside markers have added to the site's popularity and relevance in Khmer culture today.

WMF's earlier recognition of the need to prepare Preah Khan as one of many possible visitor destinations at Angkor so as to relieve pressure on the even more "charismatic" sites of Angkor Wat, the Bayon and Ta Prohm has met its objective. Within the larger scheme of things at the huge Angkor archaeological park it is increasingly clear that having a variety of visitation possibilities is good for Angkor as a whole, including for its visitors. It is mainly for this reason that WMF accepted offers to work at its three other conservation projects at Angkor: the temple of Ta Som (since 1998), the southeast gallery at Angkor Wat (since 2002) and Phnom Bakheng (since 2004). Certainly the WMF field programme at Angkor has benefited from the experience of working on these several magnificent sites simultaneously, as have the projects themselves, since lessons learned at some have benefited all.

Perhaps the most promising aspects of Preah Khan's future from the standpoint of possible new developments lie in the areas of future historical and archaeological research which can be shared with the interested public. The capacities of Angkorian research in general are currently at an all-time high, and with the aid of current documentation and diagnostic methods and display techniques there is a plethora of additional possibilities for both preserving and presenting Preah Khan and other such sites in the future. Any new plans for preserving and featuring Preah Khan should assume the great importance of continued research and the dissemination of this information for its educational benefits. The areas that are least studied to date include the southern half of the site, which was cleared of its jungle overgrowth by the APSARA authority in 2005, and sub-surface archaeology in general. Systematic archaeological investigations, when embarked on at some point in the future, will probably present a new wealth of information about the material culture and life that supported Preah Khan during its more than two centuries of operation over 500 years ago.

The honour and experience of working to preserve and feature Preah Khan are at the heart of WMF's history and accomplishments and have certainly influenced the lives of most of those who have come to know the place through our efforts. In retrospect, during the two decades of WMF's involvement at Preah Khan as the organization's "flagship" conservation project at Angkor, the site has proved to be a tremendous opportunity to learn not only about this one special place but also about the other temples at Angkor, and about Khmer and South-East Asian culture in general. Preah Khan continues to fascinate the many hundreds of experts and workers active there and the supporters of the conservation project, as part of the pantheon of ancient Khmer monumental architecture and the wider range of conservation projects on which WMF is working worldwide. Such is the power of monumental religious architecture, enhanced in this instance by a beautiful tropical setting and a famed historical culture.

# Acknowledgements

Since 1989 scores of people have helped in countless ways with the field programmes of World Monuments Fund in the Kingdom of Cambodia. Gratitude is expressed here to the numerous authorities, supporters, experts and volunteers who have assisted WMF's efforts to conserve and interpret the monastic complex of Preah Khan and other field projects at Angkor.

Thanks are extended to our hosts in the Kingdom of Cambodia: His Majesty King Norodom Sihanouk, His Majesty King Norodom Sihamoni and the representative of the Cambodian Government His Excellency President Hun Sen.

In the early years of WMF's work at Preah Khan the Cambodian Ministry of Culture provided essential guidance. Special thanks are extended to Mdm. Norodom Bopha Devi, H.E. Nouth Narang, H.E. Chouch Phoeun, Messrs. Ouk Chea, Hou Loat, Pic Keo and Phoueng Sophean. Since 1995 WMF has been guided by the APSARA National Authority chaired by H.E. Vice President Sok An, and directed by H.E. Bun Narith, and his predecessor H.E. Vann Molyvann. WMF must also note the assistance of H.E. Ros Borath, Deputy General Director, and our Cambodian colleagues at the APSARA National Authority: Mdm. Mao Laar, H.E. Khoun Khunneay, H.E. Hang Peou, Mr. Ang Chulean, Mr. Hok Pengse and Mr. Lim Srou.

Thanks are extended to the UNESCO Secretariat in Phnom Penh and the Ad Hoc Advisory Group for the UNESCO International Coordinating Committee for the Safeguarding and Development of the Historic Site of Angkor. Messrs. Azedine Beschaouch, Mounir Bouchenaki, Giorgio Croci, Pierre-André Lablaude, Kenichiro Hidaka and Hiroyuki Suzuki and their colleagues have provided extraordinary guidance to the work at Angkor. Lim Bun Hok is to be complimented on his efforts to provide clear communication between the ICC and international teams working at Angkor.

WMF's project at Preah Khan was led from the earliest field mission in 1989 through 2007 by John Sanday, who brought tremendous vision and resourcefulness to the project. WMF is also grateful to Glenn Boornazian and Konstanze von zur Mühlen, who provide leadership for current work at Angkor. WMF benefitted from international expertise and thanks Andrew Dennis, Alice Harvey, Melissa Jenkins and Prasana Weerawardene, and many other professionals who provided necessary insight into the conservation and presentation of Preah Khan. Archaeologists, art historians, conservators, historians, scientists, specialists in new technology, landscape architects and planners are some of the specialists who collaborated with WMF over the course of the last 20 years, as WMF and APSARA worked

BELOW LEFT The WMF field team for Preah Khan, 1992

BELOW The Khmer field team for WMF's four projects at Angkor, 2007

on the best solutions for safeguarding and providing public access to Preah Khan. WMF would particularly like to acknowledge Fred Aldsworth, Chip Briscoe, Bruno Bruguier, Jane Clark Chermayeff, Keith Erinberg, Bernard M. Feildern, David Flory, Predrag Gavrilovic, Jill Gilmartin, Christine Hawixbrock, Yoshiaki Ishizawa, Janos Jelen, Corneille Jest, Kimball Koch, Paolo Pagnin, Charles Pepper, Frank Preusser, Valter Santoro, Kevin Lee Sarring, Michael Schuller, Caroline Schweyer, Martha Singer, Sharon Sullivan, Simon Warrack, Thomas Warscheid, Michael Winckler and Ronnie Yimsut.

WMF is committed to training Cambodian field staff and engaging them in the planning and execution of the field work. Past and present Cambodian field team members and project administrators include Cheam Phally, Chhan Chamroeun, Chhay Sot, Chiv Phirom, Chhun Soma, Hem Sinath, Hourt Sarourt, Hun Bunwat, Keo Vathana, Kousum Sarun, Lek Sareth, Meas Kim Reth, Moeun Phary, Nay Sophea, Ouch Samon, Oun Bora, Sam Kimheng, Than Monomoyith and Var Morin. Khin Po-Thai provided valuable assistance in providing expert guided tours for WMF's guests and donors. Cambodian workers, too numerous to name here, have been the mainstay of the work on the ground at Preah Khan and WMF recognizes their outstanding and loyal commitment to this work.

The Wat Bo Dance Group is thanked for enlivening special benefit events at Preah Khan during the years 1994 through 2003.

The Center for Khmer Studies continues to be an important local partner for WMF activities.

Special thanks are extended to photographers and videographers who have generously made visual resources available to WMF: Sasha Constable, Wayne Delaroche, Michael Freeman, Les Guthman, Linda Karsteter, Susan Kleinberg, Kenro Izu, Dominique Laloux and Jaroslav Poncar.

WMF Trustees and International Council Members who were especially involved and generous in their support of the Preah Khan project include J. Carter Brown, Lois and Georges de Ménil, Hester Diamond and Ralph Kaminsky, Samuel C. and Rosetta Miller, Peter Norton Family Foundation, Marilyn Perry, Rodrigo Rodriquez, H. Peter Stern and Robert W. Wilson.

WMF is grateful to the Henry Luce Foundation for its support of this volume and to the Paul Mellon Education Endowment Fund for its continuing support of WMF's Scala series. Additional donors who have made substantial gifts to the Preah Khan project include Asian Cultural Council, Sir Anthony Bamford, Selma Ertegun, Eleanor Briggs, the Brown Foundation, Connie Higginson and American Express Foundation, Mr. and Mrs. Christopher Brewer, Carnegie Corporation of New York, Virginia James, J.M. Kaplan Fund, Nancy Lasalle, the Starr Foundation, Betty Wold Johnson and Douglas Bushnell, and Andy Warhol Foundation for Visual Arts.

Donors who made substantial contributions through WMF's *Adopt-a-Garuda* programme include Mr. and Mrs. Van L. Brady, Wendy and Bob Brandow, the Farmer Family Foundation, the Ford Family Foundation, Friends of Heritage Preservation, the Andrew P. and Geraldine A. Fuller Foundation, the Bruce A. Gimbel Foundation, Cheryl Haines and Daniel J. McCoy, Mr. and Mrs. David Koehler, Mr. and Mrs. Henry R. Kravis, Mrs. Ralph Lane, Jr., the Pierre and Tanya Matisse Foundation, Gwynn Murrill, Gerald E. O'Shaughnessy, Donald I. Perry, Leon and Cynthia Polsky, the Vin and Caren Prothro Foundation, Richard N. Purington, Mr. and Mrs. Jonathan F. Rose, Mr. and Mrs. Peter Sacerdote of the Bonnie Johnson Sacerdote Foundation, Mr. and Mrs. Randall D. Smith, the Stanford University Alumni trip (March, 1999) and Richard C. Watts.

Scores of others have generously donated to WMF's programme at Preah Khan, whose support is sincerely appreciated. Without this unprecedented international support WMF could not have sustained the Preah Khan conservation programme over a 20-year period.

Virtually every member of the WMF staff has worked on aspects of WMF's programme at Angkor, and especially at Preah Khan. All have done their part to ensure that our work at the site received the professional attention and public recognition that have made Preah Khan one of the organization's most successful undertakings. They are thanked here collectively.